SANGO
(Sanngo)
DICTIONARY &
PHRASEBOOK

SANGO
(Sanngo)
DICTIONARY &
PHRASEBOOK

Compiled by

Marcel Diki-Kidiri and John Lechner

Hippocrene Books, Inc.
New York

For information, address:
HIPPOCRENE BOOKS, INC.
171 Madison Avenue
New York, NY 10016
www.hippocrenebooks.com

Book design by Lorie DeWorken, MindtheMargins.com.

Cataloging-in-Publication Data available from the Library of Congress.

ISBN: 978-0-7818-1464-5

CONTENTS

Abbreviations

adj.	adjective
adj. phr.	adjective phrase
adv.	adverb
adv. phr.	adverb phrase
conj.	conjunction
interj.	interjection
n.	noun
n. phr.	noun phrase
num.	number
prep.	preposition
prep. phr.	preposition phrase
pron.	pronoun
v.	verb
v. phr.	verb phrase

I. THE SANGO LANGUAGE

1.1. Spelling and status

Sango is currently both the national language and the first official language of the Central African Republic. It shares official language status with French, as this language inherited from colonial times is still widely used in administration, public services, school education and written communication. Spoken by almost 98% of the population, Sango is the principal means of oral communication and socialization throughout the country, making it one of the most outstanding symbols of Central African national identity.

The name of the language is written "Sango" in all documents published before 1984 which don't consider tones. In 1984, the official orthography introduced the notation of tones in the spelling. As a result, the name of the language was spelled "Sängö", with two umlauts noting mid tones, whereas "sango" (without umlauts) means "news". In 2019, the official orthography of the Sango language was improved with new sets of rules intended to reduce the high frequency of diacritics in a text. The spelling of the language name became "Sango". By now, it can be considered that "Sango" remains an exonym which can be used in texts written in a foreign language, while "Sanngo" is mandatory in any text written in Sango language.

1.2. Classification

Sango is part of the compact continuum of Ngbandi languages, which includes Dendi, Mbangi, Gbayi (or Kpatiri), Yakoma, Sango (also known as River Sango or Sango-Yakoma) and Ngbandi from Abumombanzi, the capital of the Yakoma district in the Democratic Republic of Congo. Vehicular Sango, which later became the official national language of the Central African Republic, is the result of the véhicularisation of the river language, first under the name Dendi until around 1945, and then under the name Sango when the town of Mobaye, stronghold of River Sango, became an important stopover between Bangui and Abira, and later the capital of Haut-Oubangui.

Confusing véhicularisation with creolization, the American linguist William James Samarin[1] classified Sango as a Ngbandi-based Creole (Samarin 1967), thereby misleading the Summer Institute of Linguistics (SIL) which disseminated this misclassification. Later, other linguists, including another American, Charles Henry Morill[2] (1997), have shown his classification to be

---

1. William J. Samarin 1967. *A grammar of Sango* Mouton, The Hague (Introduction).

2. MORRILL Charles H. (1997) *The Language, Culture and Society in the Central African Republic. The Emergence and Development of Sango.* Indiana University, Bloomington,

erroneous. Sango is not an Ubangian Creole as you may read it in some publications, but simply an Ubangian lingua franca of the Ngbandi continuum. Ubangian languages themselves belong to the Adamawa-Ubangian family of the Benue-Congo branch of the Niger-Congo phylum.

1.3. History

Living at the confluence of two great rivers, the Mbomu and the Wele, which merge to form the Ubangi River, the Ngbandi people are excellent with pirogues. Before the arrival of Europeans at the end of the 19th century, they were the main river transporters along the middle course of the Ubangi as far as the village of Impfondo in the Democratic Republic of Congo. Their language became the lingua franca of the river. When the Europeans arrived, accompanied by a motley crew of Africans recruited from countries they passed through, these Africans quickly learned to speak the river's lingua franca, Sango, which they opportunely used to communicate with the villagers at every port of call from Impfondo upwards.

Later, when France occupied the entire territory of the Ubangi and Chari rivers, it was the people living along the Ubangi who were first recruited as soldiers, porters, cooks, sentries. Later, missionaries (Catholics and Protestants) and mainly Portuguese trading companies followed, opening churches and stores wherever a vehicle could go. Sango thus became the main language of evangelization and popular commerce.

Finally, the emergence of radio broadcasting, with broadcasts of all kinds in Sango (news, reports, entertainment, religion, orchestras and individual stars, etc.), helped consolidate Sango's position as the nation's language. In 1963, the congress of the *Mouvement d'Évolution Sociale d'Afrique Noire (MESAN)*, a single party created by the nation's founding father, Barthélémy Boganda, established Sango as the national language and French as the official language. In 1991, the National Assembly passed a fundamental law establishing Sango as the official language alongside French. While French is mainly used in written communication and spoken in towns by educated people, Sango is spoken throughout the country by about 98% of the population. However, the Central African authorities have not shown the political will to firmly commit to reforming the school system to include the teaching of Sango.

II. THE NEW SPELLING OF SANGO

2.1. The official 1984 spelling

The official spelling of Sängö was fixed by decree by President André Kolingba. It comprises:

- 5 oral vowels (i, e, a, o, u) pronounced without sliding[3] as in "eat, bed, bat, goat, to".
- 5 nasal vowels (in, en, an, on, un)
- 26 consonants (b, d, f, g, gb, h, k, kp, l, m, mb, mv, n, nd, ng, ngb, ny, nz, p, r, s, t, v, w, y, z)
- and above all the notation of three tone levels

The high tone is marked by a circumflex accent on the vowel: *lâ* "sun", *sô* "this, that", *wâ* "fire", *tî* "of, for, to", *dû* "hole", *dê* "cold".

The middle tone is marked by an umlaut on the vowel: *mbï* "I, me" *bï* "night", *wä* "advise", *dü* "generate", *ngö* "canoe", *tënë* "speech".

The low tone, which has the highest frequency in texts, is indicated by the absence of any accent, as follows: *ba* "bend", *na* "and, with", *tara* "try", *bi* "throw", *tene* "talk".

---

3. There is no diphthong (vowel glide) in the Sango vowels.

"Sliding" tones, also called modulated tones, which begin on one pitch and end on another pitch, are notated by splitting the vowel, each part bearing the tone of its pitch, as follows:

- High-low: *bâa* "see", *sêe* "be bitter", *zûu* "go down", *lôo / rôo* "to collect", *sîin* "to be ugly".
- Low-high: *taâ* "true, truly", *laâ* "it is…", *siîn* "too much".

With these few rules of writing, if well mastered, both writer and reader can easily communicate without ambiguity (or with very little possibility of confusion). For example, it's easy to distinguish between *sängö* (with two medium tones: name of the language) and *sango* (with two low tones: news).

2.2. Problems of 1984 spelling

Low-toned vowels, i.e. without accents, account for 44 percent of vowels in a one-page text. Vowels with a circumflex or umlaut together account for the other 56 percent. This abundance of accents makes writing and reading painful. People complained, and within two years (1984-1986) many publications abandoned tone notation, though it is necessary for clear written communication in Sango. Those who are aware of the importance of tones continue to note them, but only where they think their notation is necessary, which generates a lot of arbitrary and inconsistent decisions. Finally, others put circumflex accents and umlauts on words at random, without even thinking about what they represent. The result is a messy situation in which the official 1984 spelling has gone completely astray because Sängö is not taught in school.

2.3. The official spelling reform in 2019

In 2018, the African Academy of Languages (ACALAN) created an International Commission for the Sango language, supported by the *Laboratoire de Sociodidactique et d'Etude du Plurilinguisme (LASEP)* at the University of Bangui. The Commission worked on the problem of the frequency of tones in texts, and in 2019 came up with a solution that reduces the frequency of accents in a text from 56 to 38 percent, while keeping information on tone safe. To achieve this, the Commission considered the 1984 set of spelling rules as the basic rules (BR), which apply automatically wherever no contextual rule can be applied. To these basic rules, the Commission added two groups of contextual rules (CR1 and CR2) to handle specific contexts where the use of diacritics will be extremely reduced but totally predictable.

2.3.1. Contextual rules CR1

a) When two vowels with the same high or medium tone follow each other in the same word, the vowels /o/ and /u/ are reduced to /w/, and the vowels /e/ and /i/ are reduced to /y/. Examples: *kûê* "all" is written *kwê*, *ngîâ* "laugh" is written *ngyâ*, and *kâî* "paddle" is written *kây*.

b) When the two vowels are /u/ and /i/, as in *gûî* "yam" and *kîû* "quickly pricked", the vowel following the consonant is reduced: *gwî* and *kyû*.

c) When the vowels both carry a middle tone, it is no longer necessary to place an umlaut on the vowel that is not reduced to /w/ or /y/, as the presence of the reduced vowel (w, y) is sufficient to indicate that the other vowel is also at a middle tone. Examples: *süä* "needle" is written *swa, kïön* "selfishness" is written *kyon*.

2.3.2. Contextual rules CR2

Many Sango words have the same tone on several consecutive syllables. This is called a "tonal sequence". For example:

a) A sequence of high tones: *mbâsâmbâlâ* "seven", *târârâ* "very clean", *kpângbâlâ* "flat", *sânzêrê* "guardian", *mbîrîmbîrî* "right".

b) A sequence of middle tones: *tämbülängö* "walking", *kpëngbërë* "rocky area", *tënë* "speech", *Sängö* "name of the Sango language", etc.

To reduce the accents on these words, simply indicate the beginning and the end of the tonal sequence.

c) The tonal sequence stops when it encounters an accentuated vowel (diaresis or circumflex), a word ending, or any non-alphabetic character (i.e., punctuation.)

Examples: *tonndorozôro* "tincture of iodine"; *koddoro* "country", *tennengo-ngbanga* "trial session (in a court of law)".

d) The beginning of the tonal sequence is indicated by duplicating the first letter of the consonant that begins the second syllable, as follows: *mbâssambala, târrara, kpânngbala; tammbulango, kpenngbere, tenne, Sanngo*.

In a high-tone sequence, it's necessary to place the circumflex on the first syllable of the sequence, because the absence of the circumflex is enough to indicate that it's a medium-tone sequence.

2.3.3. How to apply these rules

CR2 rules apply to the high-tone sequence from three syllables upwards, and to the mid-tone sequence from two syllables upwards. So, *kêtê* remains unchanged while *kötä* is written *kotta*.

Basic Rules (BR) are applied automatically when no context requires the application of a contextual rule. If necessary, RC1 rules are applied first, then RC2 rules. For example:

mäïngö [BR] > *mayngö* [RC1] > *maynngo* [+RC2] "growth"

2.3.4. Special rules for special cases

Special case 1.

Verbs whose first syllable ends in a nasal vowel (e.g. *hön* "to pass", *fün* "to smell", *hän* "to be relieved, to clear up" *gbian* "to change" *gbyânngbi* "to translate") take the middle tone suffix *-ngö* in the participle, like all verbs. But since here, the *n* of the nasal vowel and the *n* of the suffix already form a double *nn*, a third *n* would be too much. It's necessary to insert an *h* between the two *n*s to indicate the tonal sequence, as follows: *honhngo* "passing, passage", *funhngo* "smelling, rotten, scent", *hanhngo* "relief, clearing", *gbyanhngo* "changing", *gbyanhngbingo* "translating, translation".

Compare:

> *hö* "to kill" *honngo* "killing"
> to *hön* "to pass" *honhngo* "passing"

> *hä* "to open wide" *hanngo* "opening wide"
> to *hän* "to be relieved" *hanhngo* "a relief"

> *fü* "to sew" *funngo* "ssewing"
> to *fün* "to smell" *funhngo* "smelling".

The result is more precise writing and clearer reading.

Special case 2.

Verbs with a modulated tone (high-low / low-high) retain the double vowel in their participles when they take the suffix -*ngö*, even if the double vowel is no longer pronounced as a long vowel here. This is to avoid confusion in written texts.

Compare:

> *ba* "bend" *banngo* "bending"
> to *bâa* "see" *baanngo* "vision"

> *fa* "show, teach" *fanngo* "showing, teaching"
> to *fâa* "cut, kill" *faanngo* "cutting, killing"

> *yo* "be far/long" *yonngo* "length"
> to *yôo* "to carry" *yoonngo* "carrying"

> *tîa* "to miss" *tyanngo* "missing"
> to *tyâa* "to catch on the fly" *tyaanngo*
> "catching on the fly"; etc.

Here too, written texts are more precise and reading easier.

Special case 3.

When a word ends with /ïi/, a mid-low glide tone on vowel /i/, the complex sequence /ïi/ is replaced by a single /y/ without any change in its pronunciation. This rule is also applicable to names of countries, towns and places that show the same feature. Examples:

Sango pronunciation	Sango orthography	English
kabinïi	kabiny	restroom
pinïi	piny	tyre
resïi	resy	receipt
famïi	famy	family
kamïi	kamy	spectacles, glasses
Azïi	Azy	Asia
Alazerïi	Alazery	Algeria
Etiopïi	Etiopy	Ethiopia
Gambïi	Gamby	Gambia
Malawïi	Malawy	Malawi
Malezïi	Malezy	Malaysia
Malïi	Maly	Mali
Moritanïi	Moritany	Mauritania
Namibïi	Namiby	Namibia
Osotralïi	Osotraly	Australia
Parïi	Pary	Paris

Sango pronunciation	Sango orthography	English
Rusïi	Rusy	Russia
Tanzanïi	Tanzany	Tanzania
Tunizïi	Tunizy	Tunisia
Zambïi	Zamby	Zambia

2.4. Illustration of the economy of accents in text

Applying the spelling reform saves an additional 18 percent of the diacritics to be added to the 44 percent unmarked low tones. As a result, 62 percent of the tones in a text are not marked by an accent due to contextual rules, as shown in the word list and example text below:

1984	2019	Translation
mbâsâmbâlâ	mbâssambala	seven
âmbênî	âmmbeni	some, sometimes
mbîrîmbîrî	mbîrrimbiri	correct, right
kpângbâlâ	kpânngbala	flat
kömändëmä	kommandema	authority
päsëmä	passema	event
sükülängö	sukkulango	washing
sägbä	saggba	advertisment
tënë	tenne	speech
hïngängö	hinngango	knowledge
kpëngbërë	kpenngbere	rocky area

1984

Na ködörösêse tî Bêafrîka, yângâ tî Sängö agbû ndo kûê, me fängö-nî na dambëtï ayeke daä pëpe. Âwamändängö-mbëtï amanda nî pëpe. Asâra sï mîngi tî âzo ahînga tî sû nî pëpe. Yê ôko sô âla manda ayeke süngö Farânzi sï tôngana âla tara tî sû Sängö, âla sû nî na ândïä tî süngö-Farânzi, atâa sô âla hînga kûê atene yângâ tî ködörö ôko ôko ayeke na kodë tî süngö-lo. Täpandë nî ayeke sô kodësüngö-Anglëe ayeke ndê, kodësüngö-Zâmani ayeke ndê, sï kodësüngö-Espanyöla ayeke ndê. Lêgë-ôko, kodësüngö-Sängö ayeke ndê na terê tî lo tî Farânzi. Ayeke na ë, âWabêafrîka, tî manda nî nzönî, sï yângâ tî ködörö tî ë alîngbi tî mâi, tî gä yângâ tî sälängö kua kûê na nî na yâ tî gîgî tî fadësô. *(223 marked tones).*

2019

Na koddorosêse tî Bêafrîka, yângâ tî Sanngo agbû ndo kwê, me fanngo-nî na dambetti ayeke daä pëpe. Âwamanndango-mbetti amanda nî pëpe. Asâra sï mîngi tî âzo ahînga tî sû nî pëpe. Yê ôko sô âla manda ayeke sunngo Farânzi sï tôngana âla tara tî sû Sanngo, âla sû nî na ândya tî sunngo Farânzi, atâa sô âla hînga kwê atene yângâ tî koddoro ôko ôko ayeke na kodë tî sunngo-lo. Täpandë nî ayeke sô kodessungo-Anglëe ayeke ndê, kodessungo-Zâmani ayeke ndê, sï kodessungo-Espanyöla ayeke ndê. Lêgë-ôko, kodessungo-Sanngo ayeke ndê na terê tî lo tî Farânzi. Ayeke na ë, âWabêafrîka, tî manda nî nzönî, sï yângâ tî koddoro tî ë alîngbi tî mâi, tî gä yângâ tî sallango kua kwê na nî na yâ tî gîgî tî fadësô. *(103 marked tones, an economy of 120 diacritics).*

Translation:

In the Central African Republic, the Sango language is spoken everywhere but not taught in schools. Students don't learn it. As a result, most people don't know how to write it. The only experience they have is how to write French. So, when they want to write Sango, they apply the rules of French spelling, even though they know that each language has its own spelling rules. For example, English spelling differs from German spelling, which differs from Spanish spelling. Similarly, the spelling of Sango is different from that of French. It's up to us Central Africans to accurately learn it, so that our language can become a language suitable for all activities in today's world.

III. ELEMENTS OF SANGO GRAMMAR

3.1. Plural nouns

The plural of nouns is marked by adding the prefix *â-* to the noun:

| Singular | *zo* | a person | *kutukutu* | car |
| Plural | *âzo* | people | *âkutukutu* | cars |

When the noun is preceded by a qualifying adjective, the *â-* prefix can be attached either to the adjective alone, the first element of the nominal group, or to both the adjective and the noun.

finî kutukutu a new car   *âfinî kutukutu*   new cars

kotta nyama a big animal   *âkotta ânyama* big animals

3.2. Personal pronouns
3.2.1. The regular personal pronouns

Singular		Plural	
mbï	I, me	*ë*	we
mo	you (singular)	*ï*	you
âla	you (plural/formal)		
lo	he, him, she, her	*âla*	they, them
nï	himself, herself (indirect style)	*ânï*	themselves (indirect style)

The pronoun *âla* is used when talking to several people, or to one single person to express respect and politeness.

Regular pronouns, including plural forms, can be prefixed with *â-*, which marks the plural of nouns. Thus formed, they are used to identify a particular category of people, who are stigmatized with the demonstrative *sô* "that".

âmbï sô	people like me,	we (me and my kind),
âmo sô	people like you,	you (singular) (you and your kind),
âlo sô	people like him,	those (him and his kind),
âë sô	people like us,	we (us and our kind),
âï sô	people like you,	you (plural) (you and your kind),
ââla sô	people like those,	those (them and their kind)

3.2.2. The indefinite personal pronoun *a*

The indefinite personal pronoun *a* is used when you don't know the subject of the verb or don't want to name it. It can be replaced in the same context by *âla* "they" with the same meaning. This is why, as a pronoun, it is written separate from the verb like all pronouns. But it can only be the subject of the verb immediately following it. It is often the equivalent of passive sentences in English.

a) *A kânga kôngbâ nî awe? / Âla kanga kôngbâ nî awe?*
Is the luggage packed up? / Did they pack the luggage up?

b) *Â hûnda mo, mo zî yângâ äpe.*
If you are asked questions, don't answer. / If someone asks you questions, don't answer.

3.2.3. The pronominal prefix *a-*, a clue to the subject

When the subject of a verb is a noun or a third-person nominal group, it is linked to the verb by the pronominal prefix *a-*, a subject index that attaches to the verb. The verb is thus conjugated with its subject.

*Lâsô, âzo mîngi **a**gue na galâ **a**wara nyama avo.*
Today, a lot of people go to the market (they) find meat, (and they) buy.

Don't confuse the indefinite pronoun *a*, which is written separate from the verb, with the pronominal subject prefix *a-*, which is attached to the verb. The latter cannot freely commute with *âla*, and the subject of the verb must be worded in the sentence. Although the standard sentence pattern is Subject-Verb-Object-Complement (SVOC), in some cases, the logical subject comes after the verb, namely when the subject is a whole sentence, as follows: *Ayeke nzönî [zo asâra kua].* (lit. **It** is good [a person works]). It is good that people work.

3.2.4. The pronoun *nî*

The pronoun *nî* can perform all the functions of a noun, except as the subject of a verb. Its grammatical use is therefore directly complementary to that of the pronoun *a* seen above, and it refers exclusively to inanimate objects, somewhat like "it" in English.

1) *Nî* as a direct object complement:

   *Töngana mo yê **nî**, mo mû **nî**.*
   If you want it, (you) take it.

2) *Nî* as a circumstantial complement introduced by the preposition *na*:

   Kobêla wa laâ lo kûi na nî?
   What illness did he die of (it)?

As a noun complement, *nî* slips into a specifier status, becoming a definite marker. It is then an equivalent of the definite article in English. It should not be labelled as an article, but just as a noun specifier.

3) *Nî* as a noun specifier:

   *Âmôlengê **nî** ate nyama **nî** kwê azia gozo **nî**.*
   The children ate all the meat and left the cassava.

As adjectives and adverbs in Sango are sub-categories of the noun, when *nî* refers to an adjective, it gives expressions of selection such as: *nzönî nî* "the good", *syonî nî* "the bad", *kotta nî* "the big", *kêtê nî* "the small", etc., and with an adverb, it gives such expressions as: *kôzo nî* "(the first) first of all", *gbânî* "(the massive way) massively", *tî mbanna nî* "(for the wicked way) on purpose", *tî kêtê nî* "for the least", *tî ndângbâ nî* "for the last," etc.

3.3. Other kinds of pronouns

3.3.1. The applicative pronoun *daä/da*.

This pronoun is written *daä* or *da*, with both pronunciations accepted. It replaces the nouns of inanimate objects only in the function of a circumstantial complement of place representing a point of impact. It corresponds to "on it, at it, to it, in it".

A sûru lêgë tî tambûla daä.	*Lo tï daä töngana bubba.*
When a road is drawn, it's for walking on it.	He fell in it (the trap) like an idiot.

With certain verbs, the pronoun *daä*, as a circumstantial of place, takes on a more symbolic value, inducing some peculiar effects of meaning and shifting the pronoun towards the status of an expressive marker (or enunciative particle).

Gue daä!	Go on!
Zî mabôko tî mo daä!	Take your hand off (from it)!
Kânga daä!	Shut up!

3.3.2. The demonstrative pronoun *sô*.

The word *sô* has several statuses. It's a demonstrative pronoun, but also a noun qualifier, a clause focalizer and a conjunction. As a pronoun, it has all the functions of a noun. It is used to designate one or more things whose names are not known. It corresponds to "that, this, that one, this one, those, these".

a) *Sô* as a demonstrative pronoun:

Mângo nî abe mîngi. Sô akpêngba kêtê laâ mbï yê.
The mangoes are too ripe.
I prefer the ones that are still firm.

Sô angbâ nzönî.
This one is still good.

b) As a noun qualifier, *sô* always follows the qualified noun.

*môlengê **sô*** this child; *da **sô*** that house;
lêgë só this way, that road.

c) As a clause focalizer, *sô* occurs at the end of the clause.
It can be translated here by "given the fact that …" or
simply "as" (+ the sentence). It points out the subordinate clause event as a reference setting for the following
clause.

*Kutukutu ayeke daä **sô**, lô gue na nî sêngê.*
As the car is available, he may go with it.

d) As a conjunction, *sô* introduces a subordinate sentence. It is well translated here by "that, as".

***Sô** âla sï ndurü na da nî, âla mä toto tî ngombe.*
As they reached near to the house, they heard a
gunshot.

e) It is worth noting that a sentence introduced by the conjunction *sô* can be simultaneously emphasized by the emphasizer *sô* at its end.

Sô *mama tî môlengê nî asï awe* **sô**, *mbï lîngbi tî gue sêngê.*
As the child's mother has come, I am free to go.

3.3.3. Interrogative pronouns: *nye, ôke, lâwa.*

a) *The pronoun nye.*
Nye means "what?" when asking for an inanimate object.

Mo yê nye?	*Irri tî mo nye*
(You want what?)	(Your name (is) what?).
What do you want?	What's your name?

b) *The pronoun ôke*
It means "how many" or "how much" in some contexts. It is used to query for a number value. That's why it's used especially where a numeric value is expected.

Sembê nî afãa ôke na lêgë? How many dishes broke on the way? (lit. Dishes broke how many on the way?)

Ôke akûi ?	*Otâ akûi.*
How many are dead?	Three are dead.

c) *The pronoun lâwa, sô wa, zo wa, ndo wa*

The interrogative pronoun *lâwa* "when" is composed of the noun *lâ* "day" and the post-nominal adjective *wa* "which". It literally means "which day?". Other constructions of the same kind have not yet merged into a single word, but function similarly, such as *zo wa* "who?", *ndo wa* "where?", *sô wa* "which one?", (respectively "which person", "which place", and "which this").

3.4. Prepositions and conjunctions
3.4.1. Prepositions

a) *Preposition tî*

The preposition *tî* can be contextually translated in English as "of, for, to". It links a noun and its complement.

> *Da tî mokönzi* the house of the chief
> *Lêgë tî gala* the road to the market

It can introduce the nominal forms of a verb, namely infinite form *tî tene* to speak, and participial form *tî tennengo* speaking. The two forms are equally used after *tî*.

> *Lo gä tî bâa mo.* He comes to see you.

> *Lo kü tî baanngo mo.* He looks forward to seeing you.

In a noun phrase, if there is no noun head before *tî*, then *tî* gets a possessive value meaning "the one of N", "for N" or "as far as N is concerned". Examples:

Nyama tî ngonda laâ. (lit. Animal of bush it is)
It is a wild animal.
Tî ngonda laâ. (of the bush it is) It is a wild one.

Kutukutu tî mbï laâ. (lit. Car of me it is) It is my car.
Tî mbï laâ. (for me it is) It is mine.

b) *Preposition na*

The preposition *na* coordinates two nouns and introduces a noun phrase as circumstantial complement.

babâ na mama father and mother
mâpa na bêre bread and butter
bï na lâ night and day (= every day, all the time)
Lo gue na yakka. He has gone to the farm.
Lêgë azî na âla. A way opens for them.

c) *Preposition wala*

The preposition *wala* means "or" and it connects two noun groups or two clauses for a choice.

Mo yê susu wala nyama? Do you want fish or meat?
Mo yeke gue na yakka, wala mo yeke ngbâ na da?
Will you go to the farm, or will you stay home?

d) *Prepositions ka, me*

The preposition *ka* introduces a noun group or a clause in contrast with previous ones. It can be translated as "but", "what about", or "and," depending on the context.

Âmbâ tî mo ahön kwê awe. Ka mo? All your friends
have gone. And you? (= What about you?).
Mo vo nyama nî, ka gozo nî ayeke wa?
You have bought the meat, but where is the casava?

The preposition *me* introduces a noun group or a clause
in contrast with previous ones while expressing the dis-
appointment of the speaker.

Me mo gä äpe! But you didn't come! / But don't come.

e) *Preposition töngana*
As a preposition, *töngana* means "like, such as" and introduces a noun group.

Lo tambûla töngana mbäkôro.
He walks like an old man.

As a conjunction, it means "if / when" and introduces a
sentence.

Töngana ngû apîka, âla gbô âbongö nî na da.
If/When it rains, they / you collect all the clothes
into the house.

f) *Prepositional phrases*
Prepositional phrases are built on the following pattern:
(na) + noun + *tî* followed by a noun group. Some of
these prepositional phrases do not require the preposition *na* to start with.

na yâ tî (lit. inside of) inside
na gwenngo tî (lit. at departure of) on the departure of
na irri tî (lit. in the name of) in the name of
na pekô tî (lit. on back of) after, behind
na lêgë tî (lit. on road of) by way of, concerning
ndâli tî, tenne tî, ngbanga tî because of
tëtî for (a compact form of *tenne tî*)

Âzo akpë koddoro nî ngbanga tî birä.
People ran away from the country because of war.

Âmôlengê nî alï da hîo ngbanga tî ngûnzapä.
The children quickly ran into the house because of
the rain.

3.4.2. Conjunctions

a) *The conjunction sô.*
For the use of *sô* as a conjunction, see section 3.3.2d.

b) *The conjunction sï.*
The conjunction *sï* establishes a priority order between
what is coming before it (the left element) and what is
coming after it (the right element), in such a way that
the left element is valued, preferred and is prior to the
right element.

Âla sukûla mabôko sï âla te kôbe.
Wash your hands before you eat.

The right element can be deleted, and this emphasizes the priority of the left element as in the following example:

Âla sukûla mabôko tî âla sï.
Wash your hands first.

The left element can be deleted, and this emphasizes the subsequent feature of the right element:

Sï âla te kôbe. Then they ate. (a consecutive sentence: Only then they ate).

Several consecutive sentences can be linked using *sï* with respect to the order of their events:

Zo asâra kua sï awara nginza, sï avo na kôbe, sï abata na sewwa tî lo.
(lit. Man works then earns money, then he buys food with it, then takes care of his family).
A man works to earn money so that he can buy food and take care of his family.

c) *Conjunction kâ*

The conjunction *kâ* introduces a clause that expresses the unrealized consequence of a virtual cause. The clause expressing the virtual cause is always in Virtual Absolute mode.

Mbî hînga tenne nî, kâ mbï gä pëpe.
If I knew about it, (then) I would not come.

Mô sïgî fadë hîo, kâ mo bâa doli nî.
If you had come out quickly a while ago, you would
have seen the elephant.

d) *The conjunction andâa (kandâa, gandâa)*
The conjunction *andâa* (also pronounced *kandâa* or
gandâa) introduces a noun group or a clause that reveals
a reality the speaker did not perceive or about which
they were mistaken.

Wâlï sô akpa hömba, andâa ayeke lo pëpe.
That woman looks like my aunt, but it is not her.

Andâa mo fadë laâ? So, it was you?

e) *The conjunction ngbangatî*
The conjunction *ngbangatî* means "for fear of" whereas
the conjunction phrase *ngbanga tî sô* means "because".
Both introduce only clauses, not noun groups.

Mbäkôro atambûla yeeke ngbangatî lô tï.
An old man walks slowly (for fear of = because) he
may fall.

Tene tenne yeeke ngbangatî âzo amä mo.
Speak lower (for fear of = because) people might
hear you.

3.4.3. Conjunction phrases

a) *Conjunctive phrases built with sô*

Built on the pattern *noun + tî + sô* the conjunction phrases *ndâli tî sô, tenne tî sô, ngbanga tî sô,* introduce a causal preposition, as they all mean "because".

Âzo ague na yakka pëpe ngbanga tî sô âlâ wara syonî kâ.
People don't go to their field because they may meet with danger there.

Âmôlengê nî akpë hîo na da ngbanga tî sô ngûnzapä âpîka âla.
The children quickly run home because they have been caught in the rain.

b) *Conjunction phrases made of a short clause*

The following clauses are used as a conjunction phrase to introduce another clause as a complement of an opinion verb: *mbï tene* I say, *mo tene* you say, *lo tene* he/she says, at*ene* (it) says, *ë tene* we say, *ï tene you* (pl.) say, *atene* (they) say. The verb of the main clause must be an opinion verb such as: *bâa* see, *hînga* know, *mä* hear, *hûnga* ask; *hânda* fool, etc. And the subject must match with the clause's subject built in the conjunction phrase.

Mbï bâa mbï tene âla yeke mû takasy.
I think / thought (that = I say) you / they are taking a taxi.

Mo hînga mo tene mamâ tî mo ayeke gä.
You know (that = you say) your mother will come.

Lo bâa lo tene or *lo bâa atene âla mä sango nî awe.*
He thought (that = he says) you had heard the news.

Ë hûnda ë tene nye apasêe?
We asked (that = we say) what happened?

Ï yêda ï tene ï yê tî sâla kua nî.
You agreed (that = you (pl.) say) you want to do the job.

Âla hânda ë atene ânï yeke mû na ë mabôko.
They fooled us (that = say) they are helping us.

3.5. Adverbs

In Sango, adverbs are *a sub-category of nouns* which can qualify actions (how / when / where you do things) or the way of being (how you are), expressed by a verb. Many adverbs are also adjectives and nouns such as *nganü* "strongly, strong, strength", *pendere* "beauty, beautiful, beautifully", *syonî* "badness, bad, badly", *nzönî* "goodness, good, well".

3.5.1. Adverbs of time

In Sango, time is not at all embedded in the tense system as it is in English. It is completely expressed by an independent adverbial system, as follows:

a) Far past: *ândö, ândö-giriri, giriri*: long time ago
b) Undefined past: *lânî* any time in the past, *mbênî lâ* one day

c) Near past: *mbênî bîrï kâ* three days ago, *mbênî bîrï* two days ago, *bîrï* yesterday, *bîrï-bîrï* just yesterday, very recently, *fadë* (placed after the verb) a while ago

d) Present time: *fadesô* now, *fafadësô* immediately

e) Continuous present: *lâkwê* always

f) Near future: *fadë* (placed before the subject)

g) Undefined future: *ânde*

h) Far future: *gbândä, gbândâgbä*

3.5.2. Adverbs of manner

The most common adverbs are as follows:

bîakü	right away	*kpâa*	newly
hîanî	effectively, for sure	*kâsâ*	firmly
yeeke, yekee	slowly, smoothly	*hîo*	quickly
gbä	in vain,	*sîin*	abusively
gbânî	massively	*töngasô*	so, like this

3.5.3. Adverbs of localization

There are two genuine adverbs of localization: *ge* "here" and *kâ* "there". However, positional nouns are used with the noun definite marker *nî* to build additional localization adverbs as follows:

na li nî (on top [of] it) on the top
na pekô nî (on back [of] it) behind
na ndâ nî (on the end [of] it) at the end, finally
na gbe nî (at the bbottom [of] it) at the bottom, down
na terê nî (on side [of] it) on the side, aside
na lê nî (on the eye [of] it) on the spot, immediately

3.6. Verbal statements

3.6.1. Modes and aspects

The Sango verbal sstatement is always set in a core grid combining one of three modes and three aspects. The modes are the Real, the Injunctive and the Virtual. The aspects are the Absolute, the Accomplished and the Unaccomplished. They are combined as follows:

Real Absolute, Real Accomplished, Real Unaccomplished.

Injunctive Absolute, Injunctive Accomplished, Injunctive Unaccomplished.

Virtual Absolute, Virtual Accomplished, Virtual Unaccomplished.

Notice that time is not at all taken into consideration in the mode and aspect system. Time is expressed by a totally separate adverbial system. (See 3.5.1).

a) **Real Absolute.**

This is an unmarked tense. It suits general statements or events considered as usual or objective fact.

*Zo kwê **ate** yê na ndo kwê.*
Everyone eats at any place.

*Ndowâ **ahön** ndö nî na burü.*
It is too hot in the dry season.

*Âwasimbäfono **agä** na ngû sô mîngi.*
A lot of tourists come / have come / came this year.

b) **Real Accomplished**

In this tense, facts are presented as terminated relative to other events of the sentence or to the referential time of the sentence. The Accomplished aspect is indicated by the marker *awe* that means "finished" and that comes at the end of the sentence.

*Âmôlengê nî **ate** kôbe **awe**.*
The children have already eaten.

*Âgene tî ë **asi awe**.*
Our guests have arrived
(have finished arriving = they are there).

*Nyama nî **amü awe**.*
The meat is cooked (has finished cooking).

c) **Real Unaccomplished**

In this tense, facts are presented as not yet finished either because they are ongoing events or because they are just foreseen but not yet started. The Unaccomplished aspect is indicated by the auxiliary verb *yeke* "to be".

Ngûnzapä ayeke pika.
It is raining / It's going to rain soon.

Mbï yeke gä. I am coming / I shall come.

Lêgë ayeke zî na âla.
The road is opening to them / The road will open to
them.

d) **Injunctive Absolute**
The Injunctive Absolute is used to give orders. It differs
from a Real Absolute statement only by the fact that
the subject pronoun of the second person singular *mo*
can be deleted.

Gä! / Mo gä! Come!

All the other subject pronouns are compulsory just like
in a Real Absolute statement. Only the context can tell
if the tense is Injunctive or Real.

Ë gue ë bâa kotta zo nî.
We go and see the big man / Let's go and see the
big man.

To avoid confusion, it is always possible to use the verb
zîa "let" at the beginning of the sentence to set the Injunctive with all the other pronouns.

Zîa ë gue ë bâa kotta zo nî.
Let's go and see the big man.

e) **Injunctive Accomplished**
In this tense, orders are expected to be executed before any other consideration. The Accomplished aspect

marker *awe* is used combined with the Injunctive features, and the sentence is expected to be followed by another sentence expressing the other possible concern.

Gä awe sï ë tene tenne. Come before we talk.

Ë mä âla kwê awe sï ë tene tenne.
Let's hear them all before we talk.

f) Injunctive Unaccomplished

This tense is used when the on-going execution of an order is required as a condition for any other consideration. It is expressed with a particular syntax made of the auxiliary verb *du* "must be" + *na* "with" + the -*ngö* form of the main verb.

Du na ganngo nî sï ë gue ë kü mo.
Be on your way to come before we go and wait for you.

Âla du na sallango mbênî kua sï zo amü na âla mbênî yê tî sâra. Let them be doing some job then they will be given some tasks to do.

g) Virtual Absolute

In the Virtual mode, events are presented as potentiality, not as objective facts. It suits conditional expressions, suppositions, non-realized or non-realistic conditions for events to truly happen. So, the Virtual mode is opposed to the Real mode and is shown by a high tone on top of the subject personal pronoun or the pronominal prefix *a-*.

Ngû âpîka, mbï sîgî äpe. If it rains, I don't go out.

Mô sïgî hïo, kâ mo bâa doli nî.
If you had come out quickly, you could have seen the
elephant.

Hânge: **mô** *tï!* Be careful! You might fall!

h) **Virtual Accomplished**

This tense is used to express a fulfilled condition for
another event to happen. It combines the Virtual high
tone marker and the Accomplished marker *awe*.

Dëmba **â***bâa kôbe* **awe***, lo dö dô.*
If Dëmba sees food, he dances
(or Once Dëmba has seen food…)

Âmôlengê nî **â***te kôbe* **awe***, âla gue alanngo.*
Once the children have eaten, they go to sleep.

i) **Virtual Unaccomplished**

This tense is used to express an unlikely condition for
another event to occur. It combines the Virtual high
tone marker and the Unaccomplished syntax *du+ na +*
Verb-*ngö*.

Âlâ **du na sallango** *mbênî kua kâ zo amû na âla mbênî
yê tî sâra.* If they have been doing some job, then
they might be given some tasks to do.

Mô du na sallango da nî sï mo dema sonngo nî.
If you were building the house, then you could complain about how difficult it is.

Virtual Unaccomplished is more and more replaced by a Real Unaccomplished construction introduced by the conjunction *töngana* "if, when", or better yet by a Virtual Absolute introduced by *âdu* "should it be" a Virtual Absolute form of the verb *du* "must be", used as an introducing conjunction.

Töngana âla yeke sâra mbênî kua sï zo amû na âla mabôko.
If they are doing some work, then someone can help them.

Âdu âla yeke sâra mbênî kua, kâ âla mä sonngo-nî.
If they were doing some work, then they would feel the pain.

3.6.2. Modality phrase.

To express the modality of a sentence in Sango, an adverb or a very short clause are placed just before the clause carrying the main information of the sentence.

a) Using an adverb:
   Fôko mbï hûnzi kua sô. I must finish this work.
   (lit. *Necessarily*, I finish this work).

   Fadë lêgë azî na âla. The road will open for them.
   (lit. *Future*, the road opens for them).

b) Using a movement verb:

Lo kîri lo ga. He comes again.
(lit. *He returns* he comes).

Lo gue lo tene mvene na irri tî mbï. He lies about me.
(lit. *He goes* and lies about my name).

Lo kpë lo tene zo laâ apîka nï. He pretends he has
been bitten. (lit. *He runs* he says someone beat him).

3.6.3. Negation

a) *Negation markers*

The adverb *ên-en* means "no" whereas *pëpe/äpe* means
"not". This is the negation marker that is put after a
noun group and at the end of a clause to negate it.

Ên-en, ayeke töngasô pëpe. No, it is not like that.

Âla gä äpe. They didn't come.

b) *Negation in a sequence of clauses*

In a sequence of clauses, each clause can be negated in-
dependently by adding *pëpe* or *äpe* at the end of each of
them as needed.

Zo alï ge pëpe, sï ânzï nginza tî mo äpe. People do not
enter here, so they cannot steal your money.

Mo yêda pëpe sï lo gä pëpe sô. You did not agree, therefore she didn't come.

c) *Negation in a sentence with a modality clause*

A modality clause cannot be negated since it expresses the modality of the other clause that follows it. So, only the latter can be negated.

Lo kîri lo ga pëpe. He doesn't come again.
(lit. *He returns* he comes not).

Lo gue lo tene mvene na irri tî mbï pëpe.
He doesn't lie about me.
(lit. *He goes* and lies about my name not).

Lo kpë lo tene zo laâ apîka nï pëpe.
He doesn't pretend he has been beaten.
(lit. *He runs* he says someone beat him not).

3.6.4. Emphasis and Focus

a) *Emphasis*

To emphasize any part of speech in a verbal statement, it is enough to pronounce it a bit louder. However, to emphasize a verb, the participle of the verb is added after it as an adverb of exclusivity.

Zo kwê anyön kâwa. Everybody drinks coffee.

Zo kwê anyön kâwa nyonhngo. Everybody does drink coffee. (lit. … drink coffee drinking).

A mû munngo na mbï pëpe, mbï vo vonngo.
It was not *given* to me; I did buy it.

A whole sentence can be emphasized by putting it between the emphasizing markers *yê sô* (that thing) and *sô*. Examples:

Yê sô, *warrango-kua fadësô ayeke taâ ngangü* **sô**!
(lit. *This thing*, finding job togay is very difficult *this*!)
It is **so** difficult to find a job today, you know?

In Sango, emphasis does not displace the emphasized element, while focus displaces the focused element.

b) *Focus*

To focalize an element, you need to put the focalizer *laâ* behind it and displace the focalized noun group at the beginning of the sentence.

Mbï vo bongö sô tîtene mo fü na môlengê nî.
I bought this cloth for you to sew for the child.

Mbï laâ *mbï vo bongö sô tîtene mo fü na môlengê nî.*
It is me who bought this cloth for you to sew for the child.

Môlengê nî laâ *mbï vo bongö sô tîtene mo fü na lo.*
It is the child for whom I bought this cloth for you to sew.

Bongö sô laâ *mbï vo tîtene mo fü na môlengê nî.*
It is this piece of cloth I bought for you to sew for the child.

To bring a verb into focus, just put its participle, with all its complements if any, at the beginning of the sentence followed by the focalizer *laâ*. Example:

Vonngo bongö sô laâ *mbï vo tîtene mo fü na môlengê ni.*
(litt. It is buying that piece of cloth I buy for you to sew for the child.)
I did buy this piece of cloth for you to sew for the child.

3.7. Nominal statements

These statements are built with a noun group as center. It is noteworthy that a syntax "group" may contain only one element or even be empty.

a) One element:
Iin! Yes.
Ên-en No.
Nî? Is it so?
Iinki! What a pity!
Nzönî! Good!

b) Two elements:
Sô nzönî That is good! (lit. That good).
Sô nye? What is this?

Nî laâ It is it, *Nye laâ?* What is it?
Mbï laâ. It is me. *Susu laâ* It is a fish.

c) Three elements:

Bongo nî pendere. The piece of cloth is beautiful
(lit. cloth-the beautiful)

Yakka nî kotta. The farm is large.

Zo kwê zo. (lit: Person all person)
All human beings are human beings (= All human
beings are fundamentally equal in rights by nature).

This short outline of the grammar of Sango is not intended to be comprehensive. However, the authors did
their best to provide the reader with enough insights to
light up in him the desire to learn the Sango language
in depth.

ENGLISH-SANGO
DICTIONARY

able *(adj.)* lîngbi
about *(prep.)* tî / na ndö tî
above *(adv.)* na ndönî
academy *(n.)* kaddami
accelerator (gas pedal) *(n.)* lidöwâ
accent *(n.)* kûne gbegô
accept *(v.)* yêda / yê daä
access *(n.)* lêgë tî sï na
accident *(n.)* ndaû
accommodation *(n.)* ndo tî lanngo
account *(n.)* kônde
accountant *(n.)* wakônde
accurate *(adj.)* tï gôh
accusation *(n.)* kallamengo-zo
accuse *(v.)* kalamêe
across *(adv.)* kôro / hö na yâ tî
act *(v.)* sâra / lï
act *(n.)* lî
activist *(n.)* bazïngêlë / ngembö
activity *(n.)* kua / lî / kualî
actor *(n.)* wakualî
actual *(adj.)* tî lênî / tî fadësô / tî bîanî
add *(v.)* zîa daä
address *(n.)* lindo
administration *(n.)* lenngo
admission *(n.)* linngo
admit *(v.)* lï
adult *(n.)* kangba
advertisement *(n.)* saggba
afraid *(adj.)* mbeto / sâra mbeto
after *(adv.)* na pekô
afternoon *(n.)* pekô tî bêkombïte
again *(adv.)* mbênî

against (*prep.*) kpo / na terê tî
age (*n.*) ngû
agency (*n.*) bêndokua
agent (*n.*) wakua
agree (*v.*) yêda / yê daä
agreement (*n.*) yenngo-daä / mângbi
agriculture (*n.*) faanngo-yakka
aid (*n.*) munngo-mabôko
aid (*v.*) mû mabôko
aide (*n.*) êde
AIDS (*n.*) syonngahözo / sidäa
air (*n.*) pupu / mbö
air conditioning (*n.*) klimatîki
airline (*n.*) lêgëhurru
airplane (*n.*) laparra
airport (*n.*) gbaggba tî laparra
airport tax (*n.*) kiri tî gbaggba tî laparra
aisle (*n.*) kpângi
alarm (*n.*) irä tî bema
alcohol (*n.*) ârêge
alive (*adj.*) finî
all (*adj.*) kwê
allergy (*n.*) (…) ke (zo)
alley (*n.*) kêtê lêgë
allow (*v.*) zîa / yêda
allowed (*adj.*) a yêda
almond (*n.*) mboma
alone (*adj.*) ôko
also (*adv.*) ngâ
altar (*n.*) ötêle
alter (*v.*) buba yâ tî
altitude (*n.*) sêmenngo
aluminum foil (*n.*) kugbë tî kângbâ

always (*adv.*) lâkwê
ambassador (*n.*) walembë
ambulance (*n.*) ammbilâsi
amenities (*n.*) nzönî dutï
among (*prep.*) na poppo tî
amount (*n.*) ndoggo
and (*prep.*) na
anemic (*adj.*) tîa mênë
anesthetic (*adj.*) tî kûi terê
angry (*adj.*) na ngonzo
animal (*n.*) nyama
ankle (*n.*) gôgerê
anniversary (*n.*) yenga tî dunngo
announcement (*n.*) bingo-sango
announcer (*n.*) wasango
annual (*adj.*) tî ngû ôko
antibiotics (*n.*) gasafi
antifreeze (*n.*) gasadê
antique (*adj.*) tî ngbêre ndo
antiseptic (*n.*) gasasannzo
any (*adj.*) mbênî (…) kîrîkiri
anybody (*n.*) zo kîrîkiri
anyone (*n.*) zo kwê
anything (*n.*) yê kwê
anywhere (*n.*) ndo kwê
apartment (*n.*) kubû-yambaa
apologize (*v.*) hûnda paradôo
apology (*n.*) hunndango-paradôo
appeal (*n.*) irringo-ndo
appear (*v.*) dunda
appendicitis (*n.*) lênngere
appetite (*n.*) nzerrengo yângâ
apple (*n.*) pômo

appointment (*n.*) kunngo-kâpä / kükâpä
April (*n.*) Ngubë
architecture (*n.*) kiinngo-yê / kiinngo-da
area (*n.*) zuka
argue (*v.*) dë pa
argument (*n.*) deppa
arm (*n.*) wên
army (*n.*) larrama
around (*adv.*) nguru
arrival (*n.*) sinngo
arrest (*v.*) retêe
arrest (*n.*) rettengo
arrive (*v.*) sï
art (*n.*) fûe
arthritis (*n.*) ngäbiö
ash (*n.*) mburuwâ
ask (*v.*) hûnda
asleep (*adj.*) lanngo
aspirin (*n.*) aspirîni
assault (*v.*) dûga
assault (*n.*) dugga
assist (*v.*) mû mabôko na
assistant (*n.*) kotti-wakua
associate (*n.*) wabosso
associate (*v.*) bôso
asthma (*n.*) âsama
attack (*v.*) dûga
attack (*n.*) duggango
attorney (*n.*) Wakokö / avokäa
August (*n.*) Kûkurû
author (*n.*) Wa / wasû
authority (*n.*) kommandema
automatic (*adj.*) bîakü lo-ôko

automatic transmission (*n.*) tonngo-yê bîakü lo-ôko
automobile (*n.*) kutukutu
autumn (*n.*) ndorobugbë
available (*adj.*) ayeke daä
avenue (*n.*) balabâla
avoid (*v.*) gasa
awake (*adj.*) zîngo
away (*adv.*) kâ
axle (*n.*) wîgbê

baby (*n.*) bebëe
baby wipes (*n.*) maswar tî ngbondâ tî bebë
babysitter (*n.*) seyä
back (*n.*) pekô
backpack (*n.*) wâkadö / bozö tî pekô
bad (*adj.*) syonî
bag (*n.*) bozö
baggage (*n.*) kôngbâ
baggage check (*n.*) wese kôngbâ
bakery (*n.*) damâpa
balcony (*n.*) balakôo
ball (*n.*) balöon
banana (*n.*) fondo
bandage (*n.*) bânde
bank (*n.*) Labânge / bânge
bank account   kônde (na bânge)
bar (place for drinking) (*n.*) bâar
barber (*n.*) wafaanngo-kwayângâ / kuafëre
barrel (*n.*) tûku
barrier (*n.*) baryere
base (*n.*) mbattana
basement (*n.*) qündâ / mbattana
basin (*n.*) gbasa

basket (*n.*) sakpä
basketball (*n.*) ndembö tî sakpä
bat (animal) (*n.*) lapârângba
bat (sports equipment) (*n.*) këkpu
bath (*n.*) sukkulango-ngû
bath towel (*n.*) kotta suimëen
bathe (*v.*) sukûla ngû
bathing suit (*n.*) bongo tî sukûla ngû
bathroom (*n.*) dûsi
battery (*n.*) baterïi
battle (*n.*) tiri
be (v. / am, is, are, was, were, been) (*v.*) yeke
beach (*n.*) Kpalando / palâzi
bean (*n.*) arikôo / gbolë
beautiful (*adj.*) pendere
because of (*prep.*) ngbanga tî
become (*v.*) gä
bed (*n.*) gbogbo
bedding (*n.*) zîa na gbogbo
bedroom (*n.*) kubû(tî)lanngo
bee (*n.*) wôtoro
beef (*n.*) (nyama tî) bâgara
beer (*n.*) byêre
before (*adv.*) kôzonî
beggar (*n.*) wayonngo-mabôko
beginning (*n.*) tonngo-ndânî
behind (*prep.*) na pekô tî
believe (*v.*) mä bê
bell (*n.*) ngbonga
below (*prep.*) na gbe tî
berry (*n.*) lêbê
beverage (*n.*) nyonhngo
beware (*v.*) hânge

bible (*n.*) bîbli
bicycle (*n.*) velöo / gbâzâbängâ
big (*adj.*) kotta
bill (*n.*) mbettifûta
birth certificate (*n.*) mbettidungo
birthday (*n.*) lâdunngo
bite (*v.*) te
bitter (*adj.*) sesêe
black (*adj.*) vukö
blanket (*n.*) balangëti
bleed (*v.*) sa mênë
bless (*v.*) kü tufa
blind (*adj.*) wazibba
blister (*n.*) apûlu
blood (*n.*) mênë
blood type (*n.*) marä tî mênë
blue (*adj.*) tutûu
boarding pass (*n.*) (mbetti) kö-na-ngö
boat (*n.*) masûa
body (*n.*) terê
bomb (*n.*) bômbe
bone (*n.*) biö
bonus (*n.*) kadöo
book (*n.*) bûku
bookstore (*n.*) dakanngo-bûku
boot (*n.*) bôti
border (*n.*) maka / yângâ
bottle (*n.*) ngbennda
bottom (*n.*) gbe
box (*n.*) sandûku / boâte
box (*v.*) gü
boy (*n.*) môlengê-kôLï
boyfriend (*n.*) ndeko

brake (*n.*) ferëen
bread (*n.*) mâpa
break (*v.*) kûngbi
breakfast (*n.*) shaynngo
breathe (*v.*) wu
bribe (*v.*) pete gôro
brick (*n.*) birîki
bridge (*n.*) kpakkpa / pôon
bring (*v.*) gä na
broken (*adj.*) gbaggba
brother (*n.*) Îtä ... tî kôlï
brown (*n.*) ngbôn
building (*n.*) yongôro kotta da
bull (*n.*) kôlï-bâgara / kôlinngba
bullet (*n.*) ngandä / lê tî ngombe
bureaucracy (*n.*) kua tî biröo
bury (*v.*) lü
bus (*n.*) bîsi / kâra
bus terminal (*n.*) ndâlêgë tî bîsi
business (*n.*) buzze
busy (*adj.*) na ndö tî kua
but (*conj.*) me / ka
butcher (*n.*) busö / wakanngo-nyama
butter (*n.*) dubêre
button (*n.*) bitöon
buy (*v.*) vo

cab (*n.*) käbîni
cabinet (*n.*) babinïi
cable (*n.*) kâmba tî wên
cable TV (*n.*) kâmba tî talâtu
cafe (*n.*) kâwa
cage (*n.*) danzânge

cake (*n.*) makala
calendar (*n.*) mbetti-kâpä
call (*v.*) îri
call (*n.*) irä / irringo-ndo
camera (*n.*) kamuräa
camp (*n.*) kândo
campground (*n.*) sêse tî kândo
can (modal verb) (*v.*) lîngbi
cancel (*v.*) woza
candy (*n.*) bomböon
car (*n.*) kutukutu
card (*n.*) kârâte
carpet (*n.*) tapïi
carrot (*n.*) kärôte
carry (*v.*) yôo
cart (*n.*) pusupûsu
case (*n.*) kâa
cash (*v.*) fûta na dedêe nginza
cash (*n.*) dedêe nginza
casual (*adj.*) na sêngê bongö
cat (*n.*) nyâö
catch (*v.*) Kamâta / tyâa
cathedral (*n.*) kotta danzapä
cattle (*n.*) ânyama
cave (*n.*) gosämba / kâvo
CD (*n.*) sêdêe / CD
cement (*n.*) simäan
cemetery (*n.*) sennde
cent (*n.*) ngbangbo
center (*n.*) bêndo
century (*n.*) sêku
cereal (*n.*) lêpêrë
chain (*n.*) zingîri

chair (*n.*) ngendë
change (*v.*) sanzêe
change (*n.*) lamonëe
changing room (*n.*) käbîni tî sannzengo-bongö
chapel (*n.*) dasambêla
chapter (*n.*) ligbâsû
charge (*n.*) sarrazema
cheap (*adj.*) tî kêtê ngêrë
check (*v.*) wese / wesenga
check (*n.*) wessengo / wesse
check in (*n.*) weselinda
check out (*n.*) wesesîgî
checkpoint (*n.*) bawesse
cheese (*n.*) kandangûme
chef (*n.*) töwakûku
chemical (*adj.*) tî sênndami
chew (*v.*) te yâ tî
chicken (*n.*) kôndo
chief (*adj.*) tö
child (*n.*) môlengê
childcare (*n.*) battango-môlengê
chocolate (*n.*) shokoläa
choke (*v.*) wu gbä
church (*n.*) danzapä
cigarette (*n.*) sigarëti
cinema (*n.*) Sindimäa / sinimäa
cinnamon (*n.*) kanêle
circle (*n.*) gbâzâ
citizen (*n.*) wakoddoro
city (*n.*) gbatta
civilian (*n.*) sïvîli
clap (*v.*) pîka sâko
class (*n.*) kubûlikôlo

classic (*n.*) gummanda
clean (*v.*) vuru
client (*n.*) kilyaan
cliff (*n.*) derêhotto
climate (*n.*) sênduzu
climb (*v.*) me
clinic (*n.*) killinîki
clock (*n.*) mbembe
close (*adj.*) sô akânga
close (*v.*) kânga
closed (*adj.*) sô akânga
cloth (*n.*) bongö
clothing (*n.*) âbongö
club (*n.*) kunndu
clutch pedal (*n.*) pedalëe tî ammbreâzi
coast (*n.*) yânngangu
coat (*n.*) kazâka
cocoa (*n.*) kakaö
coconut (*n.*) lê tî kakaö
coffee (*n.*) kâwa
coin (*n.*) ngbenngewe
cold (*adj.*) dedêe
cold (illness) (*n.*) dê
collect (*v.*) lokôto
color (*n.*) nzorôko
comb (*n.*) suali
come (*v.*) gä
comedy (*n.*) ngyâ
comfortable (*adj.*) ndofô
commission (*n.*) tokua
communication (*n.*) tôngbi
companion (*n.*) fombâ
company (*n.*) lakoppya

compare (*v.*) hâka
compensation (*n.*) polï
complain (*v.*) dema
complicated (*adj.*) zîngîli / ngûrûngbi
compromise (*n.*) manngbingo-terê kpâkpu
computer (*n.*) kombûta
conceal (*v.*) hônde
concrete (*adj.*) bêtaâ / boro
concussion (*n.*) nzï
condom (*n.*) sosêti
conductor (*n.*) wambanngo
conference (*n.*) tôngbilö
conference room (*n.*) kubû tî tôngbilö
confirm (*v.*) kuni pekô (tî)
constipated (*adj.*) yâ (tî zo) akânga
constitution (*n.*) mamândya
consulate (*n.*) dakualembë
consult (*v.*) bâa / hûnda wanngo
contagious (*adj.*) (kobêla) sô avunga hîo
contraception (*n.*) gasa-ngo
contraceptive (*n.*) yorö tî gasa ngo
contract (*n.*) mbere
convenience store (*n.*) dangêrë tî lêgë
convenient (*v.*) asâra nzönî
cook (*n.*) watöonngo-kôbe
cook (*v.*) tôo kôbe
copy (*v.*) sû pekô
copy (*n.*) sûkô
cord (*n.*) kâmba
corn (*n.*) nzö
corner (*n.*) ngö / ngonngo
correct (*adj.*) mbîrrimbiri
corrupt (*adj.*) funngo

cosmetics (*n.*) hinibaba
cost (*n.*) ngêrë
cotton (*n.*) tukîa / kotöon
cough (*n.*) tîkö
cough syrup (*n.*) siröo tî tîkö
country (*n.*) koddoro
country code (*n.*) kôde tî koddoro
court (*n.*) dangbanga
courtesy (*n.*) yammbango-zo
cover (*n.*) yângâ / ndöbê
cover charge (*n.*) fûta tî kuvvringo
cream (*n.*) krêmo
credit (*n.*) kredïi
credit card (*n.*) kârâte tî kredïi
crime (*n.*) ginon
crowd (*n.*) gbâ tî âzo
crutches (*n.*) kpo-kekke
cry (*v.*) toto
culture (*n.*) hinngango-ndo
cup (*n.*) kopo
cure (*v.*) mü / savâa
curfew (*n.*) vînga-wâ
currency (*n.*) marä-nginza
currency exchange (*n.*) sannzengo marä-nginza
customer (*n.*) kiliyäan
customs (*n.*) duâne
customs declaration (*n.*) fanngo-yê na duâne
cut (*v.*) fâa

dairy (*n.*) wakanngo-ngûme
damage (*n.*) bubbango
dance (*n.*) dôdô / dödô
danger (*n.*) syonî

dark (*n.*) vukö
date (*n.*) kâpä
date of birth (*n.*) lâ (tî) dunngo
daughter (*n.*) môlengê-wâlï (tî)
dawn (*n.*) ndätu
day (*n.*) lâ / lanngo
daytime (*n.*) lâ
dead (*n.*) kînda / kwâ
deadline (*n.*) makalanngo
deaf (*n.*) kanngango-mê
debt (*n.*) kudda
decade (*n.*) ngû balë-ôko
December (*n.*) kakawuka
decide (*v.*) kuni pa
decision (*n.*) kunipa
deck (*n.*) gbagbara / pôon
declare (*v.*) fa / dë pa
deep (*adj.*) linngo
delay (*v.*) dâka / kîri tângo na pekô
delicious (*adj.*) logoma
deliver (*v.*) (gue)…mû na
delivery (*n.*) munngo na
demand (n.) (*n.*) kammbaga
democracy (*n.*) ngunuhalëzo
dentist (*n.*) ngangatyen / nganga-pemmbe
deny (*v.*) sira
deodorant (*n.*) yommbo
department store (*n.*) vakadangêre
departure (*n.*) gwenngo
deposit (*n.*) depöo
depot (*n.*) depöo
desert (*n.*) nyammakuru
desk (*n.*) mêzä / biröo

dessert (*n.*) desëre
destination (*n.*) bogomando
diabetes (*n.*) dyabêti
detour (*n.*) ngurrungo
diabetic (*n.*) wadyabêti
diagnosis (*n.*) fandângä
dial (*v.*) pîka sînga
dialing code (*n.*) kôdesînga
diaper (*n.*) kûshi
diarrhea (*n.*) sasa
dictate (*v.*) dë na kurru gô
dictionary (*n.*) bakarî
die (*v.*) kûi
diesel (*n.*) diezële
different (*adj.*) ndê
difficult (*adj.*) katiri
dine (*v.*) te kôbe tî lâkûi
dining room (*n.*) kubû (tî te) kôbe
dinner (*n.*) kôbe tî lâkûi
diplomat (*n.*) wadalembë
direction (*n.*) yinnda / yindä
directions (*n.*) mbella / payinnda
directory (*n.*) kurulindo
dirt (*n.*) saratëe / bibbila
dirty (*adj.*) saratëe
disability (*n.*) nzeenngo terê
disabled (*adj.*) amîngo
disagree (*v.*) kombûka
disaster (*n.*) kotta kpalle
discount (*n.*) dîri-ngêrë
disease (*n.*) kobêla
dish (*n.*) sembë
disposable (*adj.*) tî bingo-nî

dispute (*v.*) papa
district (*n.*) zuka
disturb (*v.*) daranzêe
dive (*v.*) huru atï na ngû
dizzy (*adj.*) Li tî (zo) aturnêe
do (*v.*) sâra / sâla
dock (*n.*) mbattana
doctor (*n.*) wanganga
document (*n.*) dokimäan
dog (*n.*) mbo
dollar (*n.*) doläar
domestic (*adj.*) tî yângbö
door (*n.*) yângâda
double (*adj.*) dûbli
dough (*n.*) kpatta
down (*adv.*) na gbenî
downtown (*n.*) bê-gbatta
drain (*v.*) gbôto (ngû)
drama (*n.*) kotta kpalle
drawer (*n.*) gbotto / tirwär
dress (*n.*) bongö
dress (*v.*) yü
drink (*n.*) nyonhngo
drink (*v.*) nyön
drive (*v.*) gbôto kutukutu
driver's license (*n.*) peremïi tî (gbottongo-) kutukutu
drown (*adj.*) kûi na nyonhngo-ngû
drowsy (*n.*) na lanngo na lê
drug (*n.*) maimâi
drugstore (*n.*) dayorö
drunk (*adj.*) kpâtyâ
dry (*adj.*) hollengo
dry (*v.*) hôle

dry cleaner (*n.*) masïni tî sukûla na kurru nî
dryer (*n.*) kâmba tî hôle bongö
dust (*v.*) butu
duty-free (*n.*) sân kiri
DVD (*n.*) DVD / dêvêdêe
dye (*v.*) vûko (li) / hini

ear (*n.*) mê
earache (*n.*) sonngo mê
early (*adj.*) na ndën / kôzo na tângo
earth (*n.*) sêse
earthquake (*n.*) sêse ayêngi
east (*n.*) tö
eat (*v.*) te
economy (*n.*) konnomi
education (*n.*) battabgo-môlengê
egg (*n.*) parra
eight (*n.*) meambe
eighteen (*n.*) balë-ôko na meambe
eighty (*n.*) balë-meambe
election (*n.*) vôte
electric (*adj.*) tî kuräan / tî dadä
electricity (*n.*) Kuräan / dadä
elevator (*n.*) mezûu / asansëre
eleven (*n.*) bale-ôko na ôko
e-mail (*n.*) mbetti-sînga
embassy (*n.*) dalembë
emergency (*n.*) kpëkpesë
emergency room (*n.*) kubû tî kpëkpesë
employee (*n.*) zo tî kua / wakua
employer (*n.*) patröon
empty (*adj.*) hôllolo / hollolo
end (*n.*) ndâ / wenngo

enemy (*n.*) wato
energy (*n.*) ngunu
engine (*n.*) masïni / motöro
engineer (*n.*) wasêndâ-kodëkua
English language (*n.*) yângâ tî Anglëe
engraving (*n.*) kpaka-nzerë
enough (*adv.*) alîngbi
enter (*v.*) lï
entertainment (*n.*) ngyâ
entire (*adj./adv.*) kwê
entrance (*n.*) linngo
entry (*n.*) linngo
entry visa (*n.*) vizäa tî linngo
envelope (*n.*) bozö
epileptic (*adj.*) tî kobêla tî makâko
equal (*adj.*) alîngbi terê
equipment (*n.*) gbâkkuru
escalator (*n.*) ngarangâra tî masïni
estimate (*v.*) meka na lê
ethnic (*adj.*) tî maräzo
Europe (*n.*) Potto
European (*n.*) Wapotto
evacuate (*v.*) wokoso / hasa na gîgî
even (*adj.*) lêgë-ôko / litûtu
evening (*n.*) lâkûi
event (*n.*) passema
eventually (*adv.*) lêgë âdu daä
ever (*adv.*) tî lâkwê
every (*adj.*) ôko ôko
exact (*adj.*) tï gô
examine (*v.*) wesenga / bâanga
example (*n.*) täpandë
except (*adv.*) yamba

excess (v.) sï na
exchange (v.) Tûngbi / sanzêe
exchange rate (n.) mbäli tî sannzengo
exclude (v.) Zî yamba
exhaust (n.) dûgurru
exhibit (v.) fafa
exhibit (n.) faffa
exit (n.) Siggingo / sïgî
expense (n.) kanngo-nginza
expensive (adj.) ngêrë aso
experience (n.) tara-mo-bâa
expiration date (n.) Kâpä tî kaynngo
explain (v.) fa ndâ
export (v.) kä na gîgî
express (v.) tene tenne
express train (n.) dogada tî kotta lorro
extra (adj.) mbênî
eye (n.) lê
eyeglasses (n.) taratarra tî lê

fabric (n.) bongö
face (n.) lê
fall (v.) tï
false (adj.) kpakke
family (n.) sewwa
far (adv.) yongôro kâ
fare (adj.) nzönî alîngbi
farm (n.) yakka
fast (adj.) hîo
fast food (n.) kôbe hîo
fat (n.) mafüta
father (n.) babâ
faucet (n.) robinëe

fax (*n.*) sîngasûkô
fax (*v.*) to (na) sîngasûkô
February (*n.*) Fulundïgi
fee (*n.*) fûta
feel (*v.*) mä
female (*n.*) wâlï
fence (*n.*) gbaggba
festival (*n.*) kotta matânga
fever (*n.*) dê / sonngo li
field (*n.*) yakka / zuka
fifteen (*n.*) balë-ôko na okü
fifty (*n.*) balë-okü
fig (*n.*) kuturu
fill (*v.*) sï
film (*n.*) sinimäa / sindimäa
find (*v.*) wara
finger (*n.*) litï / li tî mabôko
fire (*n.*) wâ
fire alarm (*n.*) wâ tî irä
firewood (*n.*) kekkewâ
fireworks (*n.*) tûngbi-yâ
first (*adj.*) kôzo
first-aid kit (*n.*) Gbâkkuru tî kpëkpesë
first-class (*n.*) kôzo kamâ
fish (*n.*) susu
fisherman (*n.*) waginngo-susu
fishing (*n.*) ginngo-susu
fishing rod (*n.*) kekke tî yangö
fist (*n.*) gobo
fit (*v.*) lîngbi na
fitting (*n.*) linngbingo
fitting room (*n.*) kubû tî tarrango-bongö
five (*n.*) okü

fix (*v.*) leke / kuni
flag (*n.*) bandêra
flame (*n.*) lêwâ / menngawâ
flare (*n.*) blangbi
flash (*n.*) zanngo wâ
flash photography (*n.*) munngo-fotöo na zanngo wâ
flashlight (*n.*) Zanngo wâ
flat (*adj.*) kpânngbala
flat tire (*n.*) korrongo pinïi
flavor (*n.*) nzerrengo
flea (*n.*) kete
flea market (*n.*) galâ-soazïi
flight (*n.*) hurru
flight number (*n.*) nommoro tî hurru
flood (*n.*) sukkungo ngû
floor (*n.*) sêse / etâzi
flour (*n.*) fuku
flourish (*v.*) kö ndokko
flower (*n.*) ndokko / fulële
flu (*n.*) palüh
fluent (*adv.*) torôrô / tô tô tô
fluid (*adj.*) yurrungo
flush (*v.*) gbôto ngû
fly (*v.*) huru
fly (insect) (*n.*) ngungu / nzü
fog (*n.*) mbîndä / ndanndra
folk (*adj.*) tî gira
folk art (*n.*) yêfûe tî gira
follow (*v.*) mû pekô
food (*n.*) kôbe
food poisoning (*n.*) pozzonengo-kôbe
foot (*n.*) gerê
football (soccer) (*n.*) ndembö tî gerê

footpath (*n.*) lêgë tî gerê
forehead (*n.*) ndölê
foreign (*n.*) wandê
foreign currency (*n.*) nginza tî wandê
foreign languages (*n.*) yângâkoddoro tî wandê
forest (*n.*) gbakô
forget (*v.*) girisa
forgive (*v.*) lungûla tenne na li tî (zo)
fork (*n.*) kânyâ
formal (*adj.*) tî pumbä
fortune (*n.*) mosoro
fortuneteller (*n.*) wabiandö
forty (*n.*) balë-okü
fountain (*n.*) yassa
four (*n.*) usyo
fourteen (*n.*) bale-ôko na usyö
fraud (*n.*) nzï
free (*adj.*) Yamba / sêngê / nzoô
freeze (*v.*) hole na dê
fresh (*adj.*) finî
Friday (*n.*) bïkua-okü
friend (*n.*) îtä / fombâ
front (*n.*) gbelê
front desk (*n.*) mêzä tî gbelêda
frozen (*adj.*) ahôle na dê awe
fruit (*n.*) lê tî kekke / lêkekke
fry (*v.*) yôro
fuel (*n.*) kâddawa
full (*adj.*) (sï) mêkê
fun (*n.*) ngyâ
funeral (*n.*) pumbä tî kwâ
funny (*adj.*) tî ngyâ
furnished (*adj.*) sô a mû na

furniture (*n.*) kôngbâ (tî da)
future (*n.*) gbândä

game (*n.*) ngyâ / welle
garden (*n.*) zaradäa
gas tank (*n.*) tûku tî esânzi
gasoline (*n.*) Esânzi / kâddawa
gear (*n.*) pemmbe tî vïtêsi
general (*adj.*) kwêzu
get (*v.*) wara / gä
gift (*n.*) kadöo
girl (*n.*) maseka-wâlï
girlfriend (*n.*) wâlïndeko
give (*v.*) mû na
glass (*n.*) vêre / taratarra
glasses (eye) (*n.*) tatarra / taratarra
glue (*n.*) menngbo / kôle
go (*v.*) gue
goat (*n.*) ngäsa
gold (*n.*) lôro / lôlo
good (*adj.*) nzönî
goods (*n.*) nzöyê
government (*n.*) govvoroma / ngurugbya
gram (*n.*) garâmo
grammar (*n.*) ndyayângâ
grandfather (*n.*) kötarä / tarä
grandmother (*n.*) wötarä / tarä
grape (*n.*) rezëen
grass (*n.*) pêrë
great (*adj.*) kotta nzönî
green (*n.*) ngunzä
greeting (*n.*) balaô
grocery store (*n.*) dakanngo-kâsa

ground (*n.*) sêse
ground (*adj.*) tî gbenî
group (*n.*) gbâ
guard (*n.*) gârâde
guard (*v.*) bata
guest (*n.*) gene
guide (*n.*) wambanngo
guidebook (*n.*) mbettiyinda
guilty (*n.*) wakpalle
gun (*n.*) ngombe
gym (*n.*) ndo tî ngyângunu

hair (*n.*) kwâli / kwâ tî li
half (*adj.*) ndâmbo
hall (*n.*) yâdalinngo
halt (*v.*) lutti
hand (*n.*) mabôko
handicapped (*n.*) gbabbiku
happy (*v.*) bâa nzönî
harbor (*n.*) nyötûngu
hard (*adj.*) ngangï
harm (*v.*) sâra syonî na
hat (*n.*) kpoto
hazard (*n.*) yêwaâwa
he (*pron.*) lo
head (*n.*) li
health (*n.*) sênî / hanngo-terê
health insurance (*n.*) ngbasandaû tî sênî
hear (*v.*) mä
heart (*n.*) bê
heart attack (*n.*) dûga-bê
heat (*n.*) ndowâ / wâ
heavy (*adj.*) nenêe

hello (*n.*) balaô
help (*v.*) mû mabôko (na)
herb (*n.*) pêrë
here (*adv.*) ge
heterosexual (*n.*) tî kôlï na wâlï
hey (*interj.*) hêe!
highway (*n.*) kotta lêgë
hike (*n.*) simmba
hill (*n.*) hotto
HIV (*n.*) syonngahözo / VIH
hole (*n.*) dû
holiday (*n.*) konzëe
holy (*n.*) wamokondô
home (*n.*) da
homeless (*n.*) Wurukonza / konzalonndo
honest (*n.*) boro zo
honey (*n.*) lavu
horse (*n.*) mbârrata
hospital (*n.*) danganga / lopitäni
hospitality (*n.*) warrango-gene
hostage (*n.*) otâzi
hostel (*n.*) dagene tî lêgë
hostile (*adj.*) tî wato
hot (*adj.*) wâ
hotel (*n.*) dagene / otêle
hour (*n.*) ngbonga
house (*n.*) da
how (*adv.*) töngana nye
hug (*n.*) gbunngo na kate
human (*adj.*) tî boro zo
human rights (*n.*) ângura tî zo
hundred (*n.*) ngbangbo
hungry (*adj.*) na nzara

hunt (*v.*) gi nyama
hunter (*n.*) waginngo-nyama
hurry (*n.*) lorro
hurt (*v.*) pîka na kä
husband (*n.*) kôlï

I (*pron.*) mbï
ice (*n.*) ngandä
ID card (*n.*) kârâte dantitëe
idea (*n.*) bânzä / bibê
identification (*n.*) Hinngangbingo
identify (*v.*) hîngângbi
idiom (*n.*) yângâ
if (*conj.*) âdu / töngana
ignition (*n.*) zanngo-wâ
ignore (*v.*) hînga pëpe
illegal (*adj.*) na lêgë tî ndya pëpe
illness (*n.*) kobêla
immigrant (*n.*) Waggango
immigration (*n.*) gaggango
impolite (*adj.*) kpë zo pëpe
import (*v.*) gbôto na da
income (*n.*) nginza tî kua
incorrect (*adj.*) sô ayeke na lêgë nî pëpe
individual (*adj.*) tî zo ôko
indoor (*n.*) tî yâda
inexpensive (*adj.*) tî kêtê ngêrë
infant (*n.*) forôto
infect (*v.*) wara sannzo
infected (*adj.*) sô awara sannzo
infection (*n.*) sannzo
influence (*n.*) pendâ
influenza (*n.*) palüh

information (*n.*) sango
information desk (*n.*) mêzä-sango
infrastructure (*n.*) gbesêyyagbe
inject (*v.*) kpo na tonga
injury (*n.*) kä
ink (*n.*) ngûmbetti
inn (*n.*) dagene
innocent (*n.*) mabôko-vurü
inquiry (*n.*) ginngo-ndo
insect (*n.*) nzêkkede
insect bite (*n.*) pekô-yângâ tî nzêkkede
insect repellant (*n.*) tomba-nzêkkede
inside (*adv.*) na yânî / daä
inspect (*v.*) wesenga
instant (*n.*) ndembë
institution (*n.*) daseka
insufficient (*adj.*) alîngbi pëpe
insulin (*n.*) assilîni
insult (*v.*) zonga
insurance (*n.*) ngbasandaû
international (*adj.*) tî poppokodoro
Internet (*n.*) gbândatere
interpret (*v.*) fa pekô tî
interpretation (*n.*) fanngo pekô tî
interpreter (*n.*) wafanngo-pekôtenne
intersection (*n.*) sangbi
intimate (*adj.*) tî mîtâ wanî
introduce oneself (*v.*) fa terê wanî
intruder (*n.*) wandêlïda
invite (*v.*) tîsa
iron (*n.*) wên
irritate (*v.*) zö bê / sa ngonzo
island (*n.*) zwâ

issue (*n.*) tenne / kpalle
it (*pron.*) a / nî (subject / complement)
itch (*v.*) sara
item (*n.*) lêyê
itinerary (*n.*) sêlêgë

jacket (*n.*) kazâka
jail (*n.*) kanga / dangâi
jam (*n.*) kfitïi
January (*n.*) Nyenye
jar (*n.*) kopu
jeans (*n.*) dyîni
Jew (*n.*) Zwîfu
jewelry (*n.*) nngbondö lenge
job (*n.*) kua
join (*v.*) têngbi / linda
journalist (*n.*) wasango
judge (*n.*) wafaango-ngbanga
jug (*n.*) ngbenda tî sêse
juice (*n.*) ngû tî lêkâsa
July (*n.*) Lengua
jump (*v.*) huru
jumper cables (*n.*) âkpû tî zarrango-motöro
junction (*n.*) tanngbingo
June (*n.*) Föndo
jungle (*n.*) ngonda
just (*adv.*) gôh
justice (*n.*) boro ngbanga

keep (*v.*) bata
kettle (*n.*) mberêka
key (*n.*) dafungûla / kêrrere
kick (*v.*) do

kid (*n.*) môlengê
kidnap (*n.*) munngo-zo na nzï nî
kidney (*n.*) lêlê
kill (*v.*) fâa
kilogram (*n.*) kilöo / sâkigarâmo
kilometer (*n.*) killomêtere / sâkimêtere
kind (*n.*) marä
kiss (*n.*) sunngo-yângâ
kit (*n.*) gbâkkuru
kitchen (*n.*) dakûku
knapsack (*n.*) sakpä tî pekô
knee (*n.*) likunni
knife (*n.*) känîfu
knit (*n.*) triköo
knock (*v.*) pîka
knot (*n.*) kûtu
know (*v.*) hînga

lady (*n.*) madäma
lake (*n.*) kalambo
lamb (*n.*) nyîtäba
lamp (*n.*) lalâmba
land (*n.*) sêse
lane (*n.*) kêtê lêgë
language (*n.*) yângâ
laptop (*n.*) kpâlâ kombûta
large (*adj.*) tî konnongo lê
last (*adv.*) tî kôzo
last year (*n.*) ngû tî kôzo
late (*adj.*) na pekô tângo
later (*adj.*) na pekô
laugh (*n.*) henngo-ngyâ
laundromat (*n.*) ndo tî sukkulango-bongö

laundry (*n.*) ndo tî sukkulango-bongö
lavatory (*n.*) dûshi
law (*n.*) ndya
lawyer (*n.*) wandya
layover (*n.*) kukuta
leader (*n.*) wayinnda / wayindä
league (*n.*) kunndu
learn (*v.*) manda
leather (*n.*) porro
leave (*v.*) lonndo
left (*adj.*) sô angbâ
leg (*n.*) gerê
legal (*adj.*) tî ndya
legislature (*n.*) ngoindya
lemon (*n.*) zîdro
lens (*n.*) langi
less (*adj.*) kêtê ahön
letter (*n.*) lêsû / mbetti
lettuce (*n.*) saläde
level (*n.*) ndoto
library (*n.*) dabûku
lice (*n.*) siri
license (*n.*) peremïi
lid (*n.*) yângâtawâ
lie (*v.*) tene mvene
life (*n.*) ffinî / dutï / gîgî
lift (*n.*) mezû
light (*n.*) zanngo wâ
lighting (*adj.*) zanngo wâ
like (*v.*) yê
lime (*n.*) mbamba
limit (*v.*) kpo maka
limit (*n.*) maka

lip (*n.*) porronyo
liquid (*n.*) ngû
liquor (*n.*) ngûli
list (*n.*) kuru
listen (*v.*) mä
liter (*n.*) lîtri
litter (*n.*) gbäkonza
little (*adj.*) kêtê
live (*v.*) dutï
live (*adj.*) finî / fï
liver (*n.*) bebe / bê
lizard (*n.*) kadâ
load (*v.*) damêe
load (*n.*) munna
loaf (*n.*) mâpa
loan (*n.*) kudda
loan (*v.*) dêfa
local (*adj.*) tî ndo nî
location (*n.*) fanngo-ndo / ndo
lock (*v.*) kânga
lock out (*v.*) kânga yângâda na terê tî zo
locker (*n.*) kofforo
long (*adj.*) yongôro
look (*v.*) bâa / kpa
loose (*adj.*) frukpukpu
lose (*v.*) girisa
lost (*adj.*) sô agirisa
loud (*adv.*) na nduzzu
lounge (*n.*) dalisorô
love (*n.*) yenngo-terê / ndöyê
love (*v.*) yê / yê terê
low (*adv.*) na gbe nî
lucky (*adj.*) tî passa

luggage (*n.*) kôngbâ
lunch (*n.*) kôbe tî bêkombïte / midïi

machine (*n.*) masïni
mad (*adj.*) fufulafu / fûu
maid (*n.*) wâlïkua / zo tî kua
mail (*n.*) mbetti-tokua
mail (*v.*) to mbetti
main (*adj.*) kotta
make (*v.*) sâra
man (*n.*) kôlï
mandatory (*adj.*) tî kambagä nî
manual (*n.*) bûku tî manda
many (*adj.*) mîngi
map (*n.*) limondo
marketplace (*n.*) galâ
marriage (*n.*) selêka / munngo-terê
married (*n.*) [kôlï / wâlï] tî zo
marry (*v.*) mû terê na
massage (*n.*) tokua
math (*n.*) Mâti / sênndamâti
mattress (*n.*) mataläa
maximum (*adj.*) tokkota
meal (*n.*) kôbe
measure (*n.*) lêngbi
meat (*n.*) nyama
mechanic (*n.*) sêndâmasïni
medication (*n.*) munngo-yorö
medicine (*n.*) yorö
medium (*adj.*) fö
meet (*v.*) têngbi
meeting (*n.*) bûngbi
melon (*n.*) kawoya tî Potto

melt (*adj.*) sô ayolia
member (*n.*) nyîmbâ
menstruation (*n.*) baanngo-yâ
mental (*adj.*) tî li
menu (*n.*) motarâka
merchant (*n.*) wakanngo-yê / komeresäa
message (*n.*) tokua
messenger (*n.*) watokua
metal (*n.*) wên
meter (*n.*) mêtere
microwave (*n.*) mikkorônde
midday (*n.*) bêkombïte / bêlâ
middle (*n.*) bê
midnight (*n.*) bêbï
might (*v.*) alîngbi tî du
migraine (*n.*) ngagü sonngo li
mild (*adj.*) wokkongo
military (*adj.*) tî larrama
milk (*n.*) ngûme
million (*n.*) kûtu
mine (*pron.*) tî mbï
minimum (*n.*) ndâ kêtê nî
minor (*adj.*) tî kêtê nî
minor (*n.*) angbâ môlengê
mint (*n.*) nanäa
minute (*n.*) nzîna ngbonga
mirror (*n.*) tatarra / taratarra
misunderstanding (*n.*) nango-terê nzönî pëpe
mix (*v.*) hâlîngbi / melanzêe
mobile phone (*n.*) sînga tî bozö
moment (*n.*) ndembë
Monday (*n.*) bïkua-ôko
money (*n.*) nginza

monkey (*n.*) makâko
month (*n.*) nze
monument (*n.*) kîndo / danga
moon (*n.*) nze
more (*adv.*) mbênî
morning (*n.*) ndäpêrê
mosque (*n.*) mosokëe
mosquito (*n.*) ngungu
mosquito net (*n.*) gbânda-ngungu
most (*adv.*) ahön kwê
motel (*n.*) kêtê dagene
mother (*n.*) mamâ
mother-in-law (*n.*) kôgarâ tî wâlï
motion sickness (*n.*) kobêla tî simbä
motor (*n.*) motöro
motorcycle (*n.*) kpûrû
mount (*n.*) hotto
mountain (*n.*) kotta hotto
mouse (*n.*) deku
moustache (*n.*) kwa tî porronyo
mouth (*n.*) yângâ
move (*v.*) yêngi
movie (*n.*) Sindimäa / sinimäa
Mr. (title) (*n.*) Pkr
Mrs. (title) (*n.*) Ya
Ms. (title) (*n.*) Msk
much (*adv.*) mîngi
mud (*n.*) Potopôto / popôto
mural (*adj.*) tî derêe
murder (*n.*) faanngo-zo
muscle (*n.*) sade
museum (*n.*) dambesö
mushroom (*n.*) guggu

music (*n.*) mozoko
musical instrument (*n.*) ngbengë tî mozoko
musician (*n.*) wamozoko
Muslim (*n.*) mizilïmi
mystery (*n.*) ndimâ

naked (*adj.*) ndûmbu
name (*n.*) irri
napkin (*n.*) saravëte
narrow (*adj.*) Serrengo / kpêssere
nation (*n.*) halëzo tî koddoro
native (*n.*) wakoddoro
nature (*n.*) gîgî
nausea (*n.*) bê-denngo
navigation (*n.*) mbanngo-ngö
navy (*n.*) larramangû
near (*adv.*) ndurü na
nearby (*adv.*) ndurü ge
neck (*n.*) gô
necklace (*n.*) yê tî gô
need (*v.*) bezôa
needle (*n.*) swa
neighbor (*n.*) Wandongoro
neighborhood (*n.*) ndongoro
nephew (*n.*) kôya
nerve (*n.*) sisâ
neutral (*adj.*) Sambuse / kpi
never (*adv.*) zamêe / ôko äpe
new (*adj.*) finî
New Year (*n.*) Finî Ngû
New Year's Day (*n.*) Lanngo tî Finî Ngû
New Year's Eve (*n.*) Pôsö tî Finî Ngû
news (*n.*) sango

newspaper (*n.*) mbetti-sango
next (*adj.*) tî pekô
next to (*adv.*) ndurü na
next year (*n.*) ngû tî pekô
nice (*adj.*) pendere
niece (*n.*) kôya / môlengê
night (*n.*) bï
nightlife (*n.*) gîgî tî bï
nine (*n.*) gümbâyä
nineteen (*n.*) balë-ôko na gümbâyä
ninety (*n.*) balë-gümbâyä
no (*adv.*) ên-en
noise (*n.*) toto / wûrruwuru
non-smoking (*adj.*) a nyön mânga pëpe
noodles (*n.*) makoronïi
noon (*n.*) Bêlâ / bêkombïte
normal (*n.*) na lêgë nî
north (*n.*) banga
northeast (*n.*) bangatö
northwest (*n.*) bangado
nose (*n.*) hôn
note (*n.*) mekka
nothing (*n.*) yê ôko äpe
November (*n.*) Nabanndüru
now (*adv.*) fadësô
nowhere (*adv.*) na ndo ôko äpe
nuclear (*adj.*) tî zêggbelemi
number (*n.*) Wunngo / nommoro
nun (*n.*) mamêre
nurse (*n.*) seyä
nuts (*n.*) kotta pânde

occupant (*n.*) wando

occupation (*n.*) kualî
ocean (*n.*) Yammangû / gbôngû
o'clock (*adv.*) gôh
October (*n.*) Ngberere
odor (*n.*) fïon
off (*adj./adv.*) azî daä
offend (*v.*) zonga
office (*n.*) Biröo / dakua
officer (*n.*) wadakua
official (*adv.*) na lêgë tî ndya
often (*adv.*) fânî mîngi
oil (*n.*) mafüta
OK (*interj.*) Nzönî!
old (*adj.*) ngbêre
on (*prep.*) na ndö tî
once (*adv.*) fânî ôko
one (*num.*) ôko
one-way (*n.*) sênôn ôko
onion (*n.*) zonyöon
only (*adv.*) gï
open (*v.*) zî yângâ
operator (*n.*) wabuzze
opposite (*adj.*) ga
option (*n.*) sorrongo
or (*conj.*) wala
oral (*adj.*) tî yângâ
orange (*n.*) ndîmon
orchard (*n.*) yakka tî lêkekke
orchestra (*n.*) bûngbi tî mozoko
order (instruction) (*n.*) mbella
ordinary (*adj.*) sêngê
organ (*n.*) sagbê
organic (*adj.*) tî sagbê

original (*adj.*) tî kpâa nî
other (*adj.*) mbênî ndê
ought (*v.*) du fadë
our (*adj.*) tî ë
out (*adv.*) na gîgî
outdoor (*adj.*) (na) gîgî
outdoors (*n.*) tî gîgî
outside (*n.*) gîgî
oven (*n.*) fûru
over (*prep.*) na ndöbê tî
overdose (*n.*) ahön ndönî
overnight (*adv.*) bï bï bï ndo ahän
own (*v.*) yeke na
owner (*n.*) wa
oxygen (*n.*) tâsôkö

pack (*n.*) gbâ
package (*n.*) (Kanngango) gbâ
page (*n.*) lêmbetti
paid (*adj.*) a fûta awe
pain (*n.*) pâsi
painful (*adj.*) aso
painkiller (*n.*) kâi-sonngo
pair (*n.*) ûse ûse
pajamas (*n.*) bongö tî lanngo
pan (*n.*) tawâ
pants (*n.*) patalöon
paper (*n.*) mbetti
parcel (*n.*) zukayakka
pardon (*n.*) paradôo
pardon (*v.*) mû paradôo na
parent (*n.*) babâ na mamâ / sewwa
park (*n.*) ndofono

park (*v.*) garêe
parking (*n.*) bakutu / gärâzi
parliament (*n.*) bâdahalëzo
partner (*n.*) fombâ
party (*n.*) matânga
passenger (*n.*) wasimbä
passport (*n.*) passapôro
password (*n.*) pafungûla
pasta (*n.*) makoronïi
pastry (*n.*) damakala
path (*n.*) lêgë
patience (*n.*) bêkü
patient (*n.*) Zo tî kobêla / wakoba
pavement (*n.*) bêlêgë
pay (*v.*) fûta
payment (*n.*) fûta
pea (*n.*) yäkôrâ
peace (*n.*) sîrriri
peak (*n.*) likângâ
peanuts (*n.*) kârâkö
pedal (*n.*) pedäle
pedestrian (*n.*) wagerê
pen (*n.*) kpâsû
penalty (*n.*) pinningo / penaltïi (ngyângunu)
pencil (*n.*) kësû
people (*n.*) âzo
pepper (*n.*) ndôngô
percent (*n.*) yângbangbo
perfect (*adj.*) kwê pendere
period (*n.*) ngoi
permanent (*adj.*) sêkü
permission (*n.*) peremisïon
permit (*v.*) yêda na

permit (*n.*) peremïi
person (*n.*) zo
personal (*adj.*) tî wanî
pest (*n.*) syonngan
pet (*n.*) nyama tî koddoro
petrol (*n.*) petröle
pharmacy (*n.*) dayorö
phone (*n.*) sînga
phone booth (*n.*) käbîni tî sînga
phone card (*n.*) kârâte tî sînga
phone number (*n.*) nommoro tî sînga
photograph (*n.*) wamunngo-fotöo
phrase (*n.*) penzepa
physician (*n.*) wanganga
pick (*n.*) likângâ
picnic (*n.*) tê-yâ-fono
picture (*n.*) limo
pie (*n.*) kpatta
piece (*n.*) mbâgë
pig (*n.*) koso
pigeon (*n.*) mbipa
pill (*n.*) pilîli
pillow (*n.*) koli
pipe (*n.*) pepe / tiyöo
place (*n.*) ndo
plain (*adj.*) gegere
plan (*n.*) gbarra
plane (*n.*) laparra
plant (*n.*) konngo
plastic (*n.*) nilöon
plate (*n.*) sembê
platform (*n.*) mbattana
play (*n.*) ngyâ

play (*v.*) sâra ngyâ
pleasant (*adj.*) nzerrengo
please (*n.*) gerê tî âla kwê
plug (*n.*) likpo
pocket (*n.*) bozö
poem (*n.*) pafûe
point (*n.*) pânde
poison (*n.*) susu
police (*n.*) polîsi
police station (*n.*) dapolîsi
polite (*adj.*) tî kpenngo-zo
politics (*n.*) porosö
pollution (*n.*) bibbila
pool (*n.*) pïsîni
population (*n.*) halëzo
pork (*n.*) nyama tî koso
portable (*n.*) sînga tî bozö
possibly (*adv.*) âmangêe
post office (*n.*) datokua
postage (*n.*) tokkwango-yê na datokua
postal code (*n.*) nommoro tî datokua
postbox (*n.*) kofforo tî datokua
postcard (*n.*) Kôgbô mbetti-tokua
postpone (*v.*) dâka
pot (*n.*) nduttu
potato (*n.*) bäbolo
pottery (*n.*) peteta
poultry (*n.*) âkôndo
pound (*n.*) lîvri
pound (*v.*) gü
pour (*v.*) tûku
poverty (*n.*) yerre
power (*n.*) ngunu

pray (*v.*) sambêla
prefer (*v.*) yê (…) ahön
pregnant (*adj.*) sô amë ngo / mama tî ngo
prescription (*n.*) sunngo-mbella
president (*n.*) prezidäan / gbya / tömokönzi
price (*n.*) ndoggo / ngêrë
priest (*n.*) mopêre
printer (*n.*) masïni-pette
prison (*n.*) dakânga / kânga
prisoner (*n.*) wakânga / zo tî kânga
privacy (*n.*) sêyê tî wanî
private (*adj.*) tî wanî
private property (*n.*) yê tî wanî
private room (*n.*) kubû tî wanî
prize (*n.*) ngêrë / kâmba
probably (*adv.*) âmangêe
problem (*n.*) kpalle / lökûtu
product (*n.*) yêpendâ
professional (*adj.*) tî wakodëkua
professor (*n.*) wafanngo-mbetti
profile (*n.*) pelengû
profit (*n.*) tenngo
program (*n.*) pialökua / gbarra
prohibit (*v.*) ndya ake
project (*n.*) pialö
promise (*v.*) mû zendo na
promise (*n.*) zêndo
promotion (*n.*) tunnge
pronounce (*v.*) dï / dë
proper (*adj.*) boro / tî lêgë nî
property (*n.*) yê tî wanî
prosecute (*v.*) honga (zo)
prosecution (*n.*) honngango-zo

protect (*v.*) funga
protest (*v.*) ke yângâ
Protestant (*n.*) Mä-na-bê
province (*n.*) gbekoddoro
psychologist (*n.*) wasêndâgbonngo-li
public (*adj.*) polêlê / puse
public telephone (*n.*) sînga puse
public toilet (*n.*) kabinïi puse
public transportation (*n.*) yonngo-zo puse
pudding (*n.*) popôto
pull (*n.*) pilovëre
pulse (*n.*) pikkango-bê
pump (*n.*) pômbe
punch (*v.*) dûga na gobo
puncture (*n.*) gbottongo na swa
punish (*v.*) pinîi
purchase (*v.*) vo
pure (*adj.*) pîri / bêtaâ / târrara
purple (*adj.*) dammbili
purpose (*n.*) ndâ
purse (*n.*) bozö-nginza
push (*v.*) pûsu

qualify (*v.*) lîngbi
quality (*n.*) Sêboro / kalitëe
quantity (*n.*) wunngo
quarantine (*n.*) kânga yamba
quarter (*n.*) bêndâmbo
queen (*n.*) wogbya / yagbya
query (*v.*) gi
question (*v.*) hûnda
question (*n.*) hûnda
queue (*n.*) molongö

quick (*adv.*) hîo
quiet (*adj.*) sîrriri

radio (*n.*) radio / dasînga
rail (*n.*) Kpûwên (tî lêgë)
railroad (*n.*) lêgë tî wên
rain (*n.*) ngûnzapä
rain (*v.*) (ngû) apîka
ramp (*n.*) gasatï / râmba
rape (*n.*) gba-na-sanna
rape (*v.*) gba na sanna
rapid (*adj.*) na lorro / hîo
rare (*adj.*) (warrango-nî) ngangü
rat (*n.*) deku
rate (*n.*) ngûmbâ
ratio (*n.*) rasïo
ration (*n.*) sorroka
raw (*adj.*) finî
razor (*n.*) lazwara
read (*v.*) dîko(mbetti)
ready (*adj.*) ndurü na
rear (*n.*) Pekô / ngbondâ
reason (*n.*) ndâ
reasonable (*adj.*) alîngbi na nî
rebel (*n.*) waleswa
rebellion (*n.*) leswa / lesswango
receipt (*n.*) resïi
receive (*v.*) wara
recognize (*v.*) hînga / hîngângbi
recommend (*v.*) wä (zo) na
record (*v.*) sûnga
rectangle (*n.*) kamâsyo
recycle (*v.*) kîri yâ kere

red (*adj.*) bengbä
referee (*n.*) wafaanngo-papa / wafêrrere
referee (*v.*) fâa papa
reference (*n.*) bekendâ
refrigerator (*n.*) godê / frigöo
refuge (*n.*) ndokpê
refugee (*n.*) wakpê
refund (*v.*) kîri nginza
refund (*n.*) kîri-nginza
regime (*n.*) mbatê
region (*n.*) vakando
registration (*n.*) sunngango
regular (*adj.*) tî lêgë nî
relationship (*n.*) Sêtângbi / sêsewwa
relative (*n.*) sewwa
reliable (*adj.*) sô zo alîngbi tî zîa bê daä
religion (*n.*) nzapä
remedy (*n.*) yorö
remember (*v.*) dä bê na
remind (*v.*) dä bê (tî zo) na
remove (*v.*) lungûla
rent (*v.*) Zîa na luemäa
rent (*n.*) nginza tî luemäa
repair (*v.*) leke pekô tî
repair shop (*n.*) barra tî lekkengo-yê
repay (*v.*) kîri fûta
repayment (*n.*) kirringo-fûta
repeat (*v.*) kîri (mo) [+verb]
replace (*v.*) sanzêe / tûngbi
reply (*v.*) kîri yângâ
report (*v.*) tondo
reporter (*n.*) watonndo
republic (*n.*) koddorosêse

request (*v.*) hûnda

request (*n.*) hûnda

require (*v.*) hûnda

rescue (*n.*) munngo-mabôko

reservation (*n.*) piabattango

reserve (*n.*) gotanga

reservoir (*n.*) gogbâ

respect (*n.*) kpenngo-zo

respect (*v.*) kpë zo

rest (*v.*) wu terê

restaurant (*n.*) dakôbe / datenngo-kôbe

restricted (*adj.*) serêe

resume (*v.*) kîri daä

retrieve (*v.*) kîri (mo) wara

return (*v.*) kîri

reverse (*v.*) turunêe

revive (*v.*) kîri (mo) fi

revolution (*n.*) tunngbingo-sê

rib (*n.*) biö tî kate

ribbon (*n.*) Kpâlâ kâmba

rice (*n.*) lôso

ride (*v.*) kpë na mbârrata

right (*adj.*) mbîrrimbiri

right (*n.*) ngura

ring (jewelry) (*n.*) binngi

ring (sound) (*n.*) ngêrêngö

ring (*v.*) toto

riot (*n.*) leswa

rip (*v.*) sûru

risk (*n.*) rîski / tarakwâ

river (*n.*) ngû

road (*n.*) lêgë

road map (*n.*) limo-lêgë

roasted (*adj.*) zonngo
rob (*n.*) nzï
robber (*n.*) wanzï / zo tî nzï
rock (*n.*) têmë
rock (*v.*) yêngi
romance (*n.*) byâ tî bolingo
romantic (*adj.*) tî bolingo
roof (*n.*) lida / li tî da
room (*n.*) yâda / kubû
room rate (*n.*) ngêrë tî kubû
room service (*n.*) sarawîsi tî kubû
rope (*n.*) kpû / kâmba
rot (*n.*) funhngo (yê)
rotten (*adj.*) funhngo
rough (*adj.*) katiri
round-trip (*n.*) gue-mo-gä
round-trip ticket (*n.*) mbetti-lêgë tî gue-mo-gä
route (*n.*) sêlêgë
royalty (*n.*) sêgbya
rubber (*n.*) ndembö / kausüu
rude (*adj.*) sân kamenne
rug (*n.*) tapïi
ruins (*n.*) gbaggbara (da / ndo)
rule (*n.*) laggerema
run (*v.*) kpë

sacred (*adj.*) ndê
sad (*adj.*) na pâsi na bê
saddle (*n.*) mbatta
safe (*adj.*) na sîrriri
safety (*n.*) battango sîrriri
sail (*v.*) mba masûa
salad (*n.*) saläde

salary (*n.*) fûta tî kua
sale (*n.*) kanngo
sales receipt (*n.*) tikëe tî kêsi
sales tax (*n.*) Kiri tî kanngo-yê
salon (*n.*) dalisoro / dalisorô
salt (*n.*) hîngö
same (*adj.*) ôko
sample (*n.*) täpandë
sanction (*n.*) pinningo
sanctuary (*n.*) ndo-mokondô
sand (*n.*) mbuttu
sandals (*n.*) kpâkayâo
sandwich (*n.*) mâpa-na-kâsa
sanitary napkin (*n.*) kugbë tî kabinïi
satellite (*n.*) sattelîti
Saturday (*n.*) lâpôso
sauce (*n.*) ngû tî kâsa
sausage (*n.*) sosisöon
save (*v.*) sö / bata
saw (*n.*) sîi
say (*v.*) tene
scanner (*n.*) eskanëre
scar (*n.*) tokka
scare (*v.*) sâa mbeto
scarf (*n.*) batagô / bongo tî gô
scary (*adj.*) tî mbeto
scene (*n.*) lêngbadrâ
scenery (*n.*) sêlêngbandrâ
schedule (*n.*) piagbarra
school (*n.*) dambetti
science (*n.*) sênndaye
scissors (*n.*) sizöo
score (*n.*) mârâke

score (*v.*) marakêe
screen (*n.*) kêra
screw (*n.*) vîsi
screwdriver (*n.*) gbôtovîsi
sculpture (*n.*) sennde
sea (*n.*) lamêre
seafood (*n.*) nyama tî lamêre
seam (*n.*) funngo
search (*n.*) ginngo-ndo
search (*v.*) gi ndo
seasick (*n.*) bêlonndo tî lamêre
season (*n.*) ngoi
seasonal (*adj.*) tî ngoi
seasoning (*n.*) nzerekâsa
seat (*n.*) kitî
seat belt (*n.*) gbêkitî
seat number (*n.*) nommoro tî kitî
second (time) (*n.*) yakerre ngbonga
second (*num.*) ûse … (nî)
secondhand store (*n.*) dakanngo-suazïi
secret (*n.*) gbemïngo
secretary (*n.*) kuasû
section (*n.*) surä / fângbi
secular (*adj.*) sêkü
security (*n.*) bata-sîrriri
sedative (*n.*) kâi-sonngo
see (*v.*) bâa
seed (*n.*) ngoangoa
seek (*v.*) gi
seem (*v.*) kpa
select (*v.*) soro
selection (*n.*) sorrongo
self-service (*n.*) saravêe-terê

sell (*v.*) kä
seminar (*n.*) kâpammanda / seminëre
senate (*n.*) senäa
senator (*n.*) senatëre
send (*v.*) to
senior (*n.*) kangba
sensitive (*adj.*) ngangü
sentence (*n.*) pande
separate (*adj.*) yamba
separate (*v.*) kângbi
September (*n.*) Mvuka
serious (*adj.*) boro / tî taâ-tenne
servant (*n.*) bôi / va
serve (*v.*) saravêe
server (*n.*) Wasarravengo / wasarawîsi
service (*n.*) sarawîsi
settlement (*n.*) senngbingo
seven (*n.*) mbâssambala / mbrâmbrâ
seventeen (*n.*) balë-ôko na mbâssambala / mbrâmbrâ
seventy (*n.*) balë-mbâssambala / balë-mbrâmbrâ
sew (*v.*) lü
sex (*n.*) pese
shampoo (*n.*) sapwen
share (*v.*) kângbi
sharp (*adj.*) sêpê
shave (*v.*) kîo kwâ
shaving cream (*n.*) savöon tî kyonngo-kwâ
she (*pron.*) lo
sheep (*n.*) täba
sheet (*n.*) daräa
shellfish (*n.*) wakyon
shelter (*n.*) dakpê
ship (*n.*) masûa

shirt (*n.*) kate-bongö
shoe (*n.*) porro
shoot (*v.*) pîka
shop (*n.*) dangêrë / magazäni
shopkeeper (*n.*) ndombe
shoplifting (*n.*) nzï-mo-kpë
shopping basket (*n.*) gue-na-galâ / sakpä tî galâ
shopping center (*n.*) kotta galâ
shore (*n.*) yângâ tî ngû
short (*adj.*) ndurü
shot (*n.*) pîka
shoulder (*n.*) ndotti
shout (*v.*) dë konngo
show (*v.*) fa
show (*n.*) fanngo
shower (*n.*) sukkulango-ngû / dûsi
shut (*v.*) kânga
sick (*adj.*) na kobêla
side (*n.*) mbâgë
sight (*n.*) baanngo-ndo
sightseeing (*n.*) baanngo-lêndo
sign (*v.*) kekere
signal (*n.*) fâ
signature (*n.*) kekkere
silver (*n.*) nginza
sing (*n.*) byâ
single (*n.*) kombammba
single (*adj.*) koiko
sink (*v.*) lï / mû ngû
sir (*n.*) pakara
siren (*n.*) mamîwatta
sister (*n.*) Îtä ... tî wâlï
sit (*v.*) dutï

six (*n.*) omenë / omanä
sixteen (*n.*) balë-ôko na omenë
sixty (*num.*) bale-omenë
size (*n.*) mbäli
skate (*n.*) zenne
skate (*v.*) zene
skin (*n.*) porro
skirt (*n.*) zîpu
skull (*n.*) biöli
sky (*n.*) nduzzu
sleep (*v.*) lanngo
sleeping bag (*n.*) bozollango
sleeping car (*n.*) käbîni-tangê
sleeping pills (*n.*) yorö tî lanngo
slow (*adv.*) yeeke / yeke-yeke
small (*adj.*) kêtê
smell (*n.*) fîon
smile (*n.*) kêtê ngyâ
smile (*v.*) hë kêtê ngyâ
smoke (*n.*) gurru
smoking (*n.*) nyonhngo-mânga
smooth (*adj.*) muen
snack (*n.*) kâi-nzara
snake (*n.*) ngbö
snow (*n.*) fukungû / nêzi
snow (*v.*) (fukungû) apîka
soap (*n.*) kpön / savôon
soccer (*n.*) ndembö tî gerê
sock (*n.*) sosêti
soft (*adj.*) wokkongo
sold (*adj.*) a kä awe
sold out (*adj.*) a kä kwê awe
soldier (*n.*) turûgu

some *(adj.)* mbênî
someone *(n.)* mbênî zo
something *(n.)* mbênî yê
son *(n.)* môlengê (… tî) kôlï
song *(n.)* byâ
soon *(adv.)* fafadë
sore *(adj.)* sonngo
sore *(n.)* sonngo terê
sorry *(n.)* paradôo
sound *(n.)* toto
soup *(n.)* ngûkâsa
sour *(adj.)* kpekpêe / kpikpîi
source *(n.)* ligbî
south *(n.)* mbongo
soy *(n.)* sozyaa
spare *(adj.)* sô a bata
spare part *(n.)* mbâgë bata-yamba
speak *(v.)* tene
special *(adj.)* kûne
speed *(n.)* lorro / sêlorro
speed limit *(n.)* maka-lorro
speedometer *(n.)* sâa-lorro
spell *(v.)* kembe
spend *(v.)* Fûta / kä nginza
spicy *(adj.)* na nzerekâsa daä
spider *(n.)* tere / dadoro
spine *(n.)* biöngongo
spoon *(n.)* papa
sport *(n.)* ngyângunu
sports *(n.)* ângyângunu
spring (season) *(n.)* konndoko
spring (water) *(n.)* sanngo ngû
spring (metal coil) *(n.)* lesöro

square (town square) (*n.*) bando
square (form) (*adj.*) karëe
stadium (*n.*) lando
staff (*n.*) wandölikua
stairs (*n.*) ngarangâra
stamp (*n.*) têmbere
stand (*n.*) gbalâka
standard (*adj.*) sêngê
start (*v.*) tö ndânî
state (*v.*) dë pa atene
station (*n.*) balutti
statue (*n.*) dongolomîso
stay (*v.*) ngbâ
steak (*n.*) nyama tî yorrongo
steal (*v.*) nzï
step (*v.*) tö tî
step (*n.*) dâdë
sterile (*adj.*) tângömbo / tôngömbo
stitch (*n.*) liswa
stolen (*adj.*) sô a nzï awe
stomach (*n.*) yâ
stone (*n.*) têmë / tênë
stop (*v.*) lutti
store (*n.*) dangêrë / magazäni
storm (*n.*) galgula
stove (*n.*) fûrudukke
straight (*adj.*) torôrô
stranger (*n.*) wandê
street (*n.*) balabâla
student (*n.*) wamannda / wamannda-ngo-mbetti
study (*v.*) manda
substitute (*v.*) tûngbi
suburb (*n.*) gbevaka

sugar (*n.*) sukâni / sûkere / ngâakô
suit (*n.*) kazâka / komblëe
suitcase (*n.*) sandûku
suite (*n.*) yâda komblëe
summer (*n.*) zonngo
sun (*n.*) lâ
sunburn (*n.*) zonngo lâ
supermarket (*n.*) kotta magazäni
supplies (*n.*) gbâkkuru
surgeon (*n.*) (nganga) wasurrungo-zo
surgery (*n.*) surrungo-zo
surname (*n.*) irri (tî zo) tî koddoro
surprise (*n.*) yeggema
surrender (*v.*) zûku to
suspect (*n.*) wagbegibê
suspect (*v.*) gï bê (na ndö tî)
swallow (*v.*) mene
swear (*v.*) dë bä
sweat (*n.*) gbikï
sweet (*adj.*) logoma
swelling (*adj.*) sukkungo
swim (*v.*) sa ngû
symbol (*n.*) fâ
symptom (*n.*) fândâ
synagogue (*n.*) sinnagôgo
syringe (*n.*) toronga
system (*n.*) sistêma

table (*n.*) mêzä / tâbolo
tag (*n.*) pelêma
take (*v.*) mû
talk (*v.*) tene
tall (*adj.*) yongôro (na nduzzu)

tampon (*n.*) tapöon
tape (*n.*) bânde
taste (*n.*) nzerrengo
tax (*v.*) zîa kiri daä
tax (*n.*) kiri
taxi (*n.*) takasîi / takisîi
tea (*n.*) sâi
teacher (*n.*) wafanngo-mbetti / wafanngo-yê
telephone (*n.*) sînga
television (*n.*) talâtu
tell (*v.*) tene
temperature (*n.*) sêndowâ
temple (*n.*) danzapä
temporary (*adj.*) hâko / tî kêtê tângo
ten (*n.*) balë-ôko
tenant (*n.*) waluemäa
tent (*n.*) tândâ
territory (*n.*) sêse
terrorist (*n.*) watumba / terro
test (*n.*) tarra
thank you (*n.*) singîla
that (*adj.*) sô
theater (*n.*) ngbadrâ
then (*adv.*) ma
there (*adv.*) kâ
they (*pron.*) âla
thief (*n.*) wanzï
thigh (*n.*) kunni
thin (*adj.*) lâmbâ / sêpelle
thing (*n.*) yê
think (*v.*) bânza / bi bê
thirsty (*adj.*) na nzara tî ngû
thirty (*n.*) balë-otâ

this (*adj.*) sô / sô ge
thought (*n.*) bibê
thousand (*num.*) sâki
threat (n.) (*n.*) bema
threaten (*v.*) bi mbeto
three (*n.*) otâ
throat (*n.*) gô
through (*adv.*) kôro / hön na yâ tî
throw (*v.*) Bi / sa
thumb (*n.*) tälitï
thunder (*n.*) bekkpa
Thursday (*n.*) Bïkua-usyo
ticket (*n.*) biyëe / tikëe
tie (*v.*) gbë
tie (*n.*) karavâte / gbëgô
time (*n.*) tângo
tip (*n.*) yângâ
tip (*v.*) tûku
tire (*v.*) nzêen
tire (*n.*) pinïi
today (*n.*) lâsô
together (*adv.*) lêgë-ôko
toilet (*n.*) dûsi / kabinïi
toilet paper (*n.*) kugbë tî kabinïi
toll (*n.*) pïpï
toll (*v.*) pîka pïpï
tomato (*n.*) tomâte
tomorrow (*n.*) kêkerêke
tonight (*adv.*) na bï sô
tool (*n.*) zutïi / yê tî kua
tooth (*n.*) pemmbe / tyen
toothache (*n.*) sonngo pemmbe
toothbrush (*n.*) borôsi tî pemmbe

toothpaste (*n.*) kpön tî pemmbe
top (*n.*) ndöbê
torture (*n.*) sanna
total (*n.*) gbânî kwê
touch (*v.*) ndû
tourist (*n.*) wasimmba
towel (*n.*) esuimëen / suimëen
town (*n.*) gbatta
trade (*n.*) kömêresa / buzze
tradition (*n.*) gira
traditional (*adj.*) tî gira / tî koddoro
trail (*n.*) kêtê lêgë
train (*n.*) trëen / kpûgada
train station (*n.*) gâra / bagada
transfer (*n.*) tunngbingo
translate (*v.*) gbyângbi
translator (*n.*) wagbyanhngbingo-sû
transplant (*n.*) gerêfe
transport (*v.*) yôo ... ague na nî
transportation (*n.*) yonngo-(zo / kûngbâ)
trap (*v.*) tyâa
trap (*n.*) kûkû / gburuga
trash (*n.*) tabî / sakpäbî
travel (*v./n.*) simba / simbä
tray (*n.*) paläa
treat (*v.*) leke / sâra
trespassing (*n.*) lingo na ngangü
trial (*n.*) ngbanga
triangle (*n.*) ngötâ
tribe (*n.*) marä
trick (*n.*) yê tî mayëre
trick (*v.*) sâra mayëre
trip (*n.*) fonno

trolley (*n.*) trolëe
trouble (*n.*) girrisango-li
truck (*n.*) kamïon
trunk (*n.*) mangbonnga
trust (*v.*) mä bê na
trust (*n.*) nango-bê
truth (*n.*) Taâ-tenne
try (*v.*) tara
true (*adj.*) taâ
Tuesday (*n.*) Bïkua-ûse
tunnel (*n.*) lêgëdû
turn (*v.*) gini
tutor (*n.*) babâ-tunnge / mamâ-tunnge
twelve (*n.*) balë-ôko na ûse
twenty (*n.*) balë-ûse
twice *adv* fânî ûse
twin (*n.*) ângbö
type (*n.*) marä
type (*v.*) pîka

umbrella (*n.*) sarala / harala
uncle (*n.*) kôya / babâ-kêtê / babâ-kotta
uncomfortable (*adj.*) sûkkpuru-sukkpuru
unconscious (*adj./adv.*) töngana kwâ
under (*prep.*) na gbe tî
underground (*n.*) gbesêse
understand (*v.*) mä
underwear (*n.*) gbe tî bongo
undo (*v.*) zâra
unfamiliar (*v.*) yeke ndê / finî
unhappy (*v.*) bê (tî zo) anzere pëpe
uniform (*n.*) maräbongö
union (*n.*) bûngbi

United States (*n.*) Âkanza Koddoro
university (*n.*) dasênndagi
unlock (*v.*) fungûla
until (*prep.*) sûsûka / asï na
unusual (*adj.*) ndê mîngi
up (*adv.*) na nduzzu
use (*v.*) sâra na
use (*n.*) kua
usual (*adj.*) tî mîngi nî

vacancy (*v.*) ndo angbâ sêngê
vacant (*adj.*) angbâ sêngê
vacation (*n.*) konzëe
vaccinate (*v.*) vakasinêe
vaccination (*n.*) vakkasinengo
vanilla (*n.*) mazende
vegetable (*n.*) kugbë tî kâsa
vegetarian (*n.*) tekugbë
vehicle (*n.*) ngbengëkpê
veil (*n.*) lafâi / ridöo / bongö
vein (*n.*) pepesisâ
v. (*n.*) palî
very (*adj./adv.*) mîngi
video (*n.*) videö
view (*n.*) baanngo-ndo
village (*n.*) koddoro
violence (*n.*) sanna
virus (*n.*) sakî / makongö
visa (*n.*) vizäa
visit (*v.*) gä / gue gene
visit (*n.*) gene
visitor (*n.*) gene
voice (*n.*) gô / gbegô

volunteer (*n.*) wanzöbê
volunteer (*v.*) yêda na nzöbê
vomit (*v.*) dë
vote (*v.*) soro / votêe

wait (*v.*) kü
wake (*v.*) zîngo
walk (*v.*) tambûla
walk (*n.*) tambûla
wall (*n.*) derêe
wallet (*n.*) kpokkolo
want (*v.*) yê
war (*n.*) birä
warm (*adj.*) wâ kêtê
warn (*v.*) zê
warning (*n.*) zenngo-ndo
wash (*v.*) sukûla
washing machine (*n.*) masïni tî sukkulango-bongö
watch (*v.*) wese
watch (*n.*) mbembe / môndoro
water (*n.*) ngû
we (*pron.*) ë
wear (*v.*) yü
weather (*n.*) lênduzzu
wedding (*n.*) munngo-terê
Wednesday (*n.*) Bïkua-otâ
week (*n.*) yenga / dimâsi
weekday (*n.*) bikua
weekend (*n.*) wikênde
weigh (*v.*) nenga / pezêe
welcome (*v.*) wara / yamba
well (interjection) (*interj.*) habe
well (*n.*) dûngu

west (*n.*) do
what (*pron.*) nye
wheat (*n.*) farïni
wheel (*n.*) gbâzâ
wheelchair (*n.*) ngendë-gbâzâ
when (*pron.*) lâwa
where (*pron.*) ndo wa
whistle (*v.*) hûru yângâ
whistle (*n.*) hurrungo-yângâ
white (*adj.*) vurü
who (*pron.*) zo wa
why (*n.*) ngbanga tî nye
wife (*n.*) wâlï tî (zo)
wild (*adj.*) tî nyamma
win (*v.*) sö benda
wind (*n.*) pupu
window (*n.*) finêtre
wine (*n.*) divëen / vêen
wing (*n.*) kpângi
winter (*n.*) burüdê
wipe (*v.*) mbôo
wire (*n.*) kâmba tî wên / wîwên
wireless Internet (*n.*) gbândatere (sân kâmba / wîwên)
wisdom (*n.*) ndarä
wise (*adj.*) tî ndarä
withdraw (*v.*) zî
withdrawal (*n.*) zinngo
without (*prep.*) sân
woman (*n.*) wâlï
wood (*n.*) kekke
woods (*n.*) gbakô
wool (*n.*) kwatäba
word (*n.*) pa / mbupa

work (*n.*) kua / kusâra
work (*v.*) sâra kua / sâra kusâra
world (*n.*) gîgî
worm (*n.*) nguzü
worry (*v.*) bê na nduzzu
worry (*n.*) panzêe / pâsi na bê
wrap (*v.*) lurêe
wrist (*n.*) ndâgobo
write (*v.*) sû
wrong (*adj.*) na lêgë nî äpe

x-ray (*n.*) mbanza-X

year (*n.*) ngû
yeast (*n.*) sakka
yell (*v.*) dë konngo
yellow (*adj.*) kambîri
yes (*n.*) iin
yesterday (*n.*) bîrï
yogurt (*n.*) yaûru
you (*pron.*) mo / ï / âla
young (*n.*) Maseka / modô
youth (*n.*) pandara / maseka

zealous (*adj.*) na donngo-terê
zero (*n.*) nîgïsi / zeröo
zipper (*n.*) zîpi
zoo (*n.*) zôo

SANGO-ENGLISH
DICTIONARY

a (*pron.*) it
a kä kwê awe (*v.phr.*) sold out
a nyön mânga pëpe (*v.phr.*) non-smoking
a yêda (*v.*) allowed
âbongö (*n.*) clothing
âdu (*conj.*) if
ahön kwê (*v.phr.*) the most
ahön ndönî (*v.phr.*) overdose
ahön ndönî (*v.phr.*) excess
Âkanza Koddoro tî Amerîka (*n.*) United States
âkôndo (*n.*) poultry
âkpû tî zarrango-motöro (*n.*) jumper cables
âla (*pron.*) they
âla (*pron.*) you
alîngbi (*v.phr.*) enough
alîngbi na nî (*v.phr.*) reasonable
alîngbi pëpe (*v.phr.*) insufficient
alîngbi terê (*v.phr.*) equal
alîngbi tî du (*v.*) might
âmangêe (*adv.*) possibly
âmangêe (*adv.*) probably
amîngo (*v.phr.*) disabled
ammbilâsi (*n.*) ambulance
ângbö (*n.*) twin
ângura tî zo (*n.*) human rights
ângyângunu (*n.*) sports
ânyama (tî zo) (*n.*) cattle
apûlu (*n.*) blister
ârêge (*n.*) alcohol
arikôo (*n.*) bean
âsama (*n.*) asthma
asansëre (*n.*) elevator
asâra nzönî (*v.phr.*) convenient

asï na (*prep.*) until
aso (*v.phr.*) painful
assilîni (*n.*) insulin
assipirîni (*n.*) aspirin
avokäa (*n.*) attorney
ayeke daä (*v.phr.*) available
azî daä (*v.phr.*) off
âzo (*n.*) people

bâa (*v.*) look
bâa (*v.*) see
bâa (*v.*) consult
bâa nzönî (*v.phr.*) happy
bâanga (*v.*) examine
baanngo-lêndo (*n.*) sightseeing
baanngo-ndo (*n.*) sight
baanngo-ndo (*n.*) view
baanngo-yâ (*n.*) menstruation
bâar (*n.*) bar (n. / place for drinking)
babâ (*n.*) father
babâ na mamâ (*n.*) parent
babâ-kêtê (*n.*) uncle
babâ-kotta (*n.*) uncle
babâ-tunnge (*n.*) tutor
bäbolo (*n.*) sweet potato
bâdahalëzo (*n.*) parliament
bagada (*n.*) train station
bâgara (nyama tî ...) (*n.*) beef
bakarî (*n.*) dictionary
bakutu (*n.*) parking
balabâla (*n.*) avenue
balabâla (*n.*) street
balaköo (*n.*) balcony

balangëti (*n.*) blanket
balaô (*n.*) greeting
balaô (*n.*) hello
balë-gümbâyä (*n.*) ninety
balë-mbâssambala (*n.*) seventy
balë-mbrâmbrâ (*n.*) seventy
balë-meambe (*n.*) eighty
balë-ôko (*n.*) ten
balë-ôko na gümbâyä (*n.phr.*) nineteen
balë-ôko na mbâssambala (*n.phr.*) seventeen
balë-ôko na mbrâmbrâ (*n.phr.*) seventeen
balë-ôko na meambe (*n.phr.*) eighteen
bale-ôko na ôko (*n.phr.*) eleven
balë-ôko na okü (*n.phr.*) fifteen
balë-ôko na omenë (*n.phr.*) sixteen
balë-ôko na ûse (*n.phr.*) twelve
bale-ôko na usyö (*n.phr.*) fourteen
balë-okü (*n.*) fifty
balë-okü (*n.*) forty
bale-omenë (*n.*) sixty
balë-otâ (*n.*) thirty
balë-ûse (*n.*) twenty
balöon (*n.*) ball
balutti (*n.*) station
bânde (*n.*) bandage
bânde (*n.*) tape
bandêra (*n.*) flag
bando (*n.*) square (town square)
banga (*n.*) north
bangado (*n.*) northwest
bangatö (*n.*) northeast
bânge (*n.*) bank
bânza (*v.*) think

bânzä (*n.*) idea
barra tî lekkengo-yê (*n.phr.*) repair shop
baryere (*n.*) barrier
bata (*v.*) guard
bata (*v.*) keep
bata (*v.*) save
batagô (*n.*) scarf
bata-sîrriri (*n.*) security
batery (*n.*) battery
battabgo-môlengê (*n.*) education
battango sîrriri (*n.*) safety
battango-môlengê (*n.*) childcare
bawesse (*n.*) checkpoint
bazîngele (*n.*) activist
bazïngêlë (*n.*) activist
bê (*n.*) heart
bê (*n.*) liver
bê (*n.*) middle
bê (tî zo) anzere pëpe (*v.phr.*) unhappy
bê na nduzzu (*v.phr.*) worry
bebe (*n.*) liver
bebëe (*n.*) baby
bêbï (*n.*) midnight
bê-denngo (*n.*) nausea
bê-gbatta (*n.*) downtown
bekendâ (*n.*) reference
bekkpa (*n.*) thunder
bêkombïte (*n.*) midday
bêkombïte (*n.*) noon
bêkü (*n.*) patience
bêlâ (*n.*) midday
bêlâ (*n.*) noon
bêlêgë (*n.*) pavement

bêlonndo tî lamêre (*n.phr.*) seasick
bema (*v.*) threaten (v.)
bemma (*n.*) threat (n.)
bêndâmbo (*n.*) quarter
bêndo (*n.*) center
bêndokua (*n.*) agency
bengbä (*adj.*) red
bêtaâ (*adj.*) pure
bêtaâ (*adj.*) real
bezôa (*v.*) need
bi (*v.*) throw
bï (*n.*) night
bi bê (*v.phr.*) think
bï bï bï ndo ahän (*n.phr.*) overnight
bi mbeto (*v.phr.*) threaten
bïakü lo-ôko (*adv.phr.*) automatic
bibbila (*n.*) dirt
bibbila (*n.*) pollution
bibê (*n.*) idea
bibê (*n.*) thought
bîbli (*n.*) bible
bïkua (*n.*) weekday
bïkua-ôko (*n.*) Monday
bïkua-okü (*n.*) Friday
bïkua-otâ (*n.*) Wednesday
Bïkua-ûse (*n.*) Tuesday
bïkua-usyo (*n.*) Thursday
bingo-sango (*n.*) announcement
binngi (*n.*) ring (jewelry)
biö (*n.*) bone
biö tî kate (*n.phr.*) rib
biöli (*n.*) skull
biöngongo (*n.*) spine

birä (*n.*) war
bîrï (*n.*) yesterday
birîki (*n.*) brick
biröo (*n.*) desk
biröo (*n.*) office
bîsi (*n.*) bus
bitöon (*n.*) button
biyëe (*n.*) ticket
blangbi (*n.*) flare
boâte (*n.*) box
bogomando (*n.*) destination
bôi (*n.*) servant
bômbe (*n.*) bomb
bomböon (*n.*) candy
bongö (*n.*) cloth
bongö (*n.*) dress
bongö (*n.*) fabric
bongö (*n.*) veil
bongo tî gô (*n.phr.*) scarf
bongö tî lanngo (*n.phr.*) pajamas
bongo tî sukûla ngû (*n.phr.*) bathing suit
boro (*adj.*) effective
boro (*adj.*) concrete
boro (zo) (*n.*) honest (person)
boro ngbanga (*n.phr.*) justice
borôsi tî pemmbe (*n.phr.*) toothbrush
bôso (*v.*) associate
bôti (*n.*) boot
bozö (*n.*) bag
bozö (*n.*) pocket
bozollango (*n.*) sleeping bag
bozö-mbetti (*n.*) envelope
bozö-nginza (*n.*) purse

buba yâ tî (*v.phr.*) alter
bubbango (*n.*) damage
bûku (*n.*) book
bûku tî manda (*n.phr.*) manual
bûngbi (*n.*) meeting
bûngbi (*v.*) unite
bûngbi (*n.*) union
bûngbi tî mozoko (*n.phr.*) orchestra
Burüdê (*n.*) winter
busö (*n.*) butcher
butu (*n.*) dust (v.)
buzze (*n.*) business
buzze (*n.*) trade
byâ (*n.*) sing
byâ (*n.*) song
byâ tî bolingo (*n.phr.*) romance (song)
byêre (*n.*) beer

da (*n.*) home
da (*n.*) house
dä bê (tî zo) na (*v.phr.*) remind
dä bê na (*v.phr.*) remember
daä (*adv.*) on it
dabûku (*n.*) library
dadä (*n.*) electricity
dâdë (*n.*) step
dadoro (*n.*) spider
dafungûla (*n.*) key
dagene (*n.*) hotel
dagene (*n.*) inn
dagene tî lêgë (*n.phr.*) hostel
dâka (*v.*) postpone
dakânga (*n.*) prison

dakanngo-bûku (*n.*) bookstore
dakanngo-kâsa (*n.*) grocery store
dakanngo-suazy (*n.*) secondhand store
dakka (*v.*) delay
dakôbe (*n.*) restaurant
dakpê (*n.*) shelter
dakua (*n.*) office
dakualembë (*n.*) consulate
dakûku (*n.*) kitchen
dalembë (*n.*) embassy
dalisoro (*n.*) living room
dalisorô (*n.*) lounge
dalisorô (*n.*) living room
damakala (*n.*) pastry
damâpa (*n.*) bakery
dambesö (*n.*) museum
dambetti (*n.*) school
damêe (*v.*) load
dammbili (*adj.*) purple
danga (*n.*) villa
dangâi (*n.*) jail
danganga (*n.*) hospital
dangbanga (*n.*) court
dangêrë (*n.*) shop
dangêrë (*n.*) store
dangêrë tî lêgë (*n.phr.*) convenience store
danzânge (*n.*) cage
danzapä (*n.*) church
danzapä (*n.*) temple
dapolîsi (*n.*) police station
daräa (*n.*) sheet
daranzêe (*v.*) disturb
dasambêla (*n.*) chapel

dasekka (*n.*) institution
dasênndagi (*n.*) university
dasînga (*n.*) radio station
datenngo-kôbe (*n.*) restaurant
datokua (*n.*) post office
dayorö (*n.*) drugstore
dayorö (*n.*) pharmacy
dê (*n.*) cold (illness, weather)
dê (*n.*) fever
dë (*v.*) pronounce
dë (*v.*) vomit
dë bä (*v.phr.*) swear
dë gapa (*v.phr.*) argue
dë konngo (*v.phr.*) shout
dë na kurru gô (*v.phr.*) dictate
dë pa (*v.phr.*) declare
dë pa (*v.phr.*) state
dedêe (*adj.*) cold
dedêe nginza (*n.phr.*) cash
dêfa (*v.*) loan
deku (*n.*) mouse
deku tî ngonda (*n.phr.*) rat
dema (*v.*) complain
depöo (*n.*) deposit
depöo (*n.*) depot
deppa (*n.*) statement
deppa (*n.*) declaration
dere konngo (*v.phr.*) yell
derêe (*n.*) wall
derêhotto (*n.*) cliff
desëre (*n.*) dessert
dêvvedêe (DVD) (*n.*) DVD
dï (*v.*) pronounce

diezële (*n.*) diesel
dîko(mbetti) (*v.*) read
dimâsi (*n.*) week
dîri-ngêrë (*n.*) discount
divëen (*n.*) wine
do (*v.*) pull
do (*n.*) west
dö (*n.*) axe
dö (*v.*) kick
dö dô (*v.phr.*) dance (*v.*)
dôdô (*n.*) dance (*n.*)
dödô (*n.*) dance (*n.*)
dogada tî kotta lorro (*n.phr.*) express train
dokimäan (*n.*) document
doläar (*n.*) dollar
dongolomîso (*n.*) statue
donngo-terê (*n.*) zealousness
du (*v.*) must be
dû (*n.*) hole
du fadë (*v.phr.*) ought
duâne (*n.*) customs
dubêre (*n.*) butter
dubli (*v.*) double (*v.*)
dûbli (*adj.*) double
dûga (*v.*) assault
dûga (*v.*) attack
dûga na gobo (*v.phr.*) punch
dûga-bê (*n.*) heart attack
dugga (*n.*) assault
duggango (*n.*) attack
dûgurru (*n.*) exhaust
dunda (*v.*) appear
dûngu (*n.*) well

dûsi (*n.*) lavatory
dûsi (*n.*) shower
dûsi (*n.*) toilet
dûsi (*n.*) bathroom
dutï (*n.*) life
dutï (*v.*) live
dutï (*v.*) sit
dyabêti (*n.*) diabetes
dyîni (*n.*) jeans

ë (*pron.*) we
êde (*n.*) aide
ên-en (*adv.*) no
esânzi (*n.*) gasoline
eskanëre (*n.*) scanner
esuimëen (*n.*) towel
etâzi (*n.*) floor (from first up)

fa (*v.*) show
fâ (*n.*) signal
fâ (*n.*) symbol
fa ndâ (*v.phr.*) explain
fa pekô tî (*v.phr.*) interpret
fa terê wanî (*v.phr.*) introduce oneself
fâa (*v.*) cut
fâa (*v.*) kill
fâa papa (*v.*) referee
faanngo-yakka (*n.*) agriculture
faanngo-zo (*n.*) murder
fadësô (*adv.*) now
fafa (*v.*) exhibit
fafadë (*adv.*) quite soon
faffa (*n.*) exhibit

fandâ (*n.*) symptom
fandângä (*n.*) diagnosis
fângbi (*n.*) section
fânî mîngi (*adv.phr.*) often
fânî ôko (*adv.phr.*) once
fânî ûse (*adv.phr.*) twice
fanngo (*n.*) show
fanngo pekô tî (*n.phr.*) interpretation
fanngo pekô tî (*n.phr.*) relating (narration)
fanngo-ndo (*n.*) showing a place
fanngo-yê na duâne (*n.phr.*) customs declaration
farïni (*n.*) wheat
ferëen (*n.*) brake
fî (*adj.*) live
finêtre (*n.*) window
finî (*n.*) life
finî (*adj.*) alive
finî (*adj.*) fresh
finî (*adj.*) live
finî (*adj.*) new
finî (*adj.*) raw
Finî Ngû (*n.*) New Year
fîon (*n.*) odor
fîon (*n.*) smell
fö (*adj.*) medium
fombâ (*n.*) companion
fombâ (*n.*) friend
fombâ (*n.*) partner
fondo (*n.*) banana
Föndo (*n.*) June
fonno (*n.*) trip
fono (*v.*) take a walk
forôto (*n.*) infant

frigöo (*n.*) refrigerator
frukpukpu (*adj.*) loose
fü (*v.*) sew
fûe (*n.*) art
fufulafu (*n.*) madness
fuku (*n.*) flour
fukungû (*n.*) snow
fulële (*n.*) flower
Fulundïgi (*n.*) February
funga (*v.*) protect
fungûla (*v.*) unlock
funhngo (*adj.*) rotten
funhngo (*adj.*) corrupt
funhngo yê (*n.phr.*) rot
funngo (*n.*) seam
fûru (*n.*) oven
fûrudukke (*n.*) stove
fûta (*n.*) fee
fûta (*v.*) pay
fûta (*n.*) payment
fûta na dedêe nginza (*v.phr.*) pay cash
fûta nginza (*v.phr.*) spend
fûta tî kua (*n.phr.*) salary
fûta tî kuvvringo (*n.phr.*) cover charge
fûu (*n.*) madness

ga (*n.*) opposite
gä (*v.*) become
gä (*v.*) come
gä (*v.*) get (+adj)
gä gene (*v.phr.*) visit (come as a guest)
gä na (*v.*) bring
gaggango (*n.*) immigration

galâ (*n.*) marketplace
galâ-soazy (*n.*) flea market
galgula (*n.*) storm
gapa (*n.*) argument
gâra (*n.*) train station
gârâde (*n.*) guard
garâmo (*n.*) gram
gärâzi (*n.*) parking
garêe (*v.*) park
gasa (*v.*) avoid
gasadê (*n.*) antifreeze
gasafi (*n.*) antibiotics
gasa-ngo (*n.*) contraception
gasa-sannzo (*n.*) antiseptic
gasa-tinngo (*n.*) ramp
gbâ (*n.*) pack
gbâ (*n.*) group
gba na sanna (*v.phr.*) rape (*v.*)
gbâ tî âzo (*n.phr.*) crowd
gbabbiku (*n.*) handicapped
gbagbara (*n.*) deck
gbaggba (*adj.*) broken
gbaggba (*n.*) fence
gbaggba tî laparra (*n.phr.*) airport
gbaggbara (*adj.*) wrecked
gbaggbara (da/ndo) (*n.phr.*) ruins
gbâkkuru (*n.*) equipment
gbâkkuru (*n.*) kit
gbâkkuru (*n.*) supplies
gbâkkuru tî kpëkpesë (*n.phr.*) first-aid kit
gbakô (*n.*) forest
gbakô (*n.*) woods
gbäkonza (*n.*) worn mat

gbalâka (*n.*) stand
gba-na-sanna (*n.*) rape (*n.*)
gbândä (*n.*) future
gbândangungu (*n.*) mosquito net
gbândatere (*n.*) Internet
gbândatere sân kâmba (*n.phr.*) wireless Internet
gbânî kwê (*n.phr.*) total
gbarra (*n.*) plan
gbarra (*n.*) program
gbasa (*n.*) basin
gbatta (*n.*) city
gbatta (*n.*) town
gbâzâ (*n.*) circle
gbâzâ (*n.*) wheel
gbâzâbängâ (*n.*) bicycle
gbe (*n.*) bottom
gbê (*n.*) link
gbê (*n.*) knut
gbë (*v.*) tie
gbe tî bongo (*n.phr.*) underwear
gbegô (*n.*) voice
gbëgô (*n.*) tie
gbêkitî (*n.*) seat belt
gbekoddoro (*n.*) province
gbelê (*n.*) front
gbemïngo (*n.*) secret
gbesêse (*n.*) underground
gbesêyyagbe (*n.*) infrastructure
gbevaka (*n.*) suburb
gbikï (*n.*) sweat
gbogbo (*n.*) bed
gbolë (*n.*) bean
gbôngû (*n.*) ocean

gbôto (ngû) (*v.phr.*) drain
gbôto kutukutu (*v.phr.*) drive
gbôto na da (*v.phr.*) import
gbôto ngû (*v.*) flush
gbôto-vîsi (*n.*) screwdriver
gbotto (*n.*) drawer
gbottongo na swa (*n.phr.*) puncture
gbunngo na kate (*n.phr.*) hug
gburuga (*n.*) trap
gbya (*n.*) president
gbyângbi (*v.*) translate
ge (*adv.*) here
gegere (*adj.*) plain
gene (*n.*) guest
gene (*n.*) visit
gene (*n.*) visitor
gerê (*n.*) leg
gerê (*n.*) foot
gerê tî âla kwê (*n.phr.*) please
gerêfe (*n.*) transplant
gi (*v.*) query
gi (*v.*) seek
gï (*adv.*) only
gi bê (na ndö tî) (*v.phr.*) suspect
gi ndo (*v.phr.*) search
gi nyama (*v.phr.*) hunt
gîgî (*n.*) life
gîgî (*n.*) nature
gîgî (*n.*) outside
gîgî (*n.*) world
gîgî tî bï (*n.phr.*) nightlife
gini (*v.*) turn
ginngo-ndo (*n.*) inquiry

ginngo-ndo (*n.*) search
ginngo-susu (*n.*) fishing
ginnho-nyama (*n.*) hunting
ginon (*n.*) crime
gira (*n.*) tradition
girisa (*v.*) forget
girisa (*v.*) lose
girrisango-li (*n.*) oblivion
gô (*n.*) neck
gô (*n.*) throat
gô (*n.*) voice
gobo (*n.*) fist
godê (*n.*) refrigerator
gogbâ reservoir
gôgerê (*n.*) ankle
gôh (*adv.*) just
gôh (*adv.*) o'clock
gosämba (*n.*) cave
gotanga (*n.*) reserve
govvoroma (*n.*) government
gü (*v.*) box (*v.*)
gü (*v.*) pound
gue (*v.*) go
gue (...) mù na (*v.phr.*) deliver
gue gene (*v.phr.*) visit (go as a guest)
gue-mo-gä (*n.*) round-trip
gue-na-galâ (*n.*) shopping basket
guggu (*n.*) mushroom
gümbâyä (*n.*) nine
gummanda (*n.*) classic
gündâ (*n.*) root
gurru (*n.*) smoke
gwenngo (*n.*) departure

habe (*interj.*) well
hâka (*v.*) compare
hâko (*adj.*) temporary
halëzo (*n.*) population
halëzo tî koddoro (*n.phr.*) nation
hâlîngbi (*v.*) mix
hânge (*v.*) beware
hanngo-terê (*n.*) health
harala (*n.*) umbrella
hasa na gîgî (*v.phr.*) excavate
hë kêtê ngyâ (*v.phr.*) smile (*v.*)
hêe! (*interj.*) hey
henngo-ngyâ (*n.*) laugh
hînga (*v.*) know
hînga (*v.*) recognize
hînga pëpe (*v.phr.*) ignore
hîngângbi (*v.*) recognize
hîngângbi (*v.*) identify
hîngângbi (*v.*) recognize
hîngânzi (*v.*) identify
hîngö (*n.*) salt
hinibaba (*n.*) cosmetics
hinngangbingo (*n.*) identification
hinngango-ndo (*n.*) culture
hîo (*adv.*) fast
hîo (*adv.*) quick
hîo (*adv.*) quickly
hôle (*v.*) dry (v.)
hôle na dê (*v.*) freeze
hollengo (*adj.*) dry (*adj.*)
hollolo (*adj.*) empty
hôllolo (*adj.*) empty
hôn (*n.*) nose

hön na yâ tî (*v.phr.*) through (go through)
hön na yâ tî (*v.phr.*) across (go through)
hônde (*v.*) conceal
honga (zo) (*v.*) prosecute
honngango-zo (*n.*) prosecution
hotto (*n.*) hill
hotto (*n.*) mount
hûnda (*v.*) ask
hûnda (*v.*) question
hûnda (*n.*) question
hûnda (*v.*) request
hûnda (*n.*) request
hûnda (*v.*) require
hûnda paradôo (*v.phr.*) apologize
hûnda wanngo (*v.*) consult
hunndango-paradôo (*n.*) apology
hurru (*n.*) flight
hurrungo-yângâ (*n.*) whistle
huru (*v.*) fly
huru (*v.*) jump
hûru (*v.*) blow
huru (...) tï na ngû (*v.phr.*) dive
hûru yângâ (*v.phr.*) whistle

ï (*pron.*) you (plural)
iin (*n.*) yes
irä (*n.*) call (for help)
irä tî bema (*n.*) alarm
îri (*v.*) call (v.)
irri (*n.*) name
irri (tî zo) tî koddoro (*n.*) surname
irringo-ndo (*n.*) appeal
irringo-ndo (*n.*) call (n.)

îtä (*n.*) sibbling
îtä (*n.*) friend
Îtä tî (zo) tî kôlï (*n.phr.*) brother
Îtä tî (zo) tî wâlï (*n.phr.*) sister

ka (*conj.*) but
kâ (*adv.*) away
kâ (*adv.*) there
kä (*n.*) injury
kä (*v.*) sell
kä na gîgî (*v.phr.*) export
kä nginza (*v.phr.*) spend
kâa (*n.*) case
käbîni (*n.*) office (professional)
käbîni (*n.*) cab
käbîni tî sannzengo-bongö (*n.phr.*) changing room
käbîni tî sînga (*n.phr.*) phone booth
käbîni-tangê (*n.*) sleeping car
kabiny (*n.*) toilet cabinet
kabiny (*n.*) toilet
kabiny puse (*n.phr.*) public toilet
kadâ (*n.*) lizard
kaddami (*n.*) academy
kâddawa (*n.*) fuel
kâddawa (*n.*) gasoline
kadöo (*n.*) bonus
kadöo (*n.*) gift
kâi-nzara (*n.*) snack
kâi-sonngo (*n.*) painkiller
kâi-sonngo (*n.*) sedative
kakaö (*n.*) cocoa
Kakawuka (*n.*) December
kalambo (*n.*) lake

kalamêe (*v.*) accuse
kalitëe (*n.*) quality
kallamengo-zo (*n.*) accusation
kamâsyo (*n.*) rectangle
kamâta (*v.*) catch
kâmba (*n.*) cord
kâmba (*n.*) prize
kâmba (*n.*) rope
kâmba tî hôle bongö (*n.phr.*) dryer
kâmba tî talâtu (*n.phr.*) cable TV
kâmba tî wên (*n.phr.*) cable
kâmba tî wên (*n.*) wire
kambaga (*v.*) demand (*v.*)
kambîri (*adj.*) yellow
kameräa (*n.*) camera
kamïon (*n.*) truck
kammbaga (*n.*) demand (*n.*)
kandangûme (*n.*) cheese
kândo (*n.*) camp
kanêle (*n.*) cinnamon
kânga (*n.*) jail
kânga (*v.*) close
kânga (*v.*) lock
kânga (*n.*) prison
kânga (*v.*) shut
kânga yamba (*v.phr.*) quarantine
kânga yângâda na li tî zo (*v.phr.*) lock (someone) in
kânga yângâda na terê tî zo (*v.phr.*) lock (someone) out
kangba (*n.*) adult
kangba (*n.*) senior
kângbi (*v.*) separate
kângbi (*v.*) share
känîfu (*n.*) knife

kanngango gbâ (*n.phr.*) package
kanngango-mê (*n.*) deaf
kanngo (*n.*) sale
kanngo-nginza (*n.*) expense
kânyâ (*n.*) fork
kâpä (*n.*) date
kâpä tî kaynngo (*n.phr.*) expiration date
kâpammanda (*n.phr.*) seminar
kâra (*n.*) bus
kârâkö (*n.*) peanuts
kârâte (*n.*) card
kârâte dantitëe (*n.phr.*) ID card
kârâte tî kredy (*n.phr.*) credit card
kârâte tî sînga (*n.phr.*) phone card
karavâte (*n.*) tie
karëe (*adj.*) square (form)
kärôte (*n.*) carrot
kate-bongö (*n.*) shirt
katiri (*adj.*) difficult
katiri (*adj.*) rough
kausüu (*n.*) rubber
kâvo (*n.*) cave
kâwa (*n.*) cafe
kâwa (*n.*) coffee
kawoya tî Potto (*n.phr.*) melon
kazâka (*n.*) coat
kazâka (*n.*) jacket
kazâka (*n.*) suit
ke yângâ (*v.phr.*) protest
kekere (*v.*) sign
kêkerêke (*n.*) tomorrow
kekke (*n.*) wood
kekke tî yangö (*n.phr.*) fishing rod

kekkere (*n.*) signature
kekkewâ (*n.*) firewood
këkpu (*n.*) mortar pestle
këkpu (*n.*) bat (sports equipment)
kembe (*v.*) spell
kêra (*n.*) screen
kêrrere (*n.*) key
kësû (*n.*) pencil
kete (*n.*) flea
kêtê (*adj.*) little
kêtê (*adj.*) small
kêtê ahön (*adj.phr.*) less
kêtê dagene (*n.phr.*) motel
kêtê lêgë (*n.phr.*) alley
kêtê lêgë (*n.*) lane
kêtê lêgë (*n.phr.*) trail
kêtê ngyâ (*n.phr.*) smile
kiliyäan (*n.*) customer
killinîki (*n.*) clinic
killomêtere (*n.*) kilometer
kilöo (*n.*) kilogram
kilyaan (*n.*) client
kînda (*n.*) dead
kindo (*n.*) monument
kinngo-da (*n.*) architecture
kinngo-yê (*n.*) architecture
kîo kwa (*v.phr.*) shave
kîri (*n.*) tax
kîri (*v.*) return
kîri (mo) [+verb] (*v.phr.*) repeat
kîri (mo) fi (*v.phr.*) revive
kîri (mo) fûta (*v.phr.*) repay
kîri (mo) wara (*v.phr.*) retrieve

kîri daä (*v.phr.*) resume
kîri nginza (*v.phr.*) refund
kîri tângo na pekô (*v.phr.*) delay (purposedly)
kiri tî gbaggba tî laparra (*n.phr.*) airport tax
kiri tî kanngo-yê (*n.phr.*) sales tax
kîri yâ kere (*v.phr.*) recycle
kîri yângâ (*v.phr.*) reply
kîri-nginza (*n.*) refund (*n.*)
kirringo-fûta (*n.*) repayment
kitî (*n.*) seat
klimatîki (*n.*) air conditioning
kö ndokko (*v.*) flourish
kôbe (*n.*) food
kôbe (*n.*) meal
kôbe hîo (*n.phr.*) fast food
kôbe tî bêkombïte (*n.phr.*) lunch
kôbe tî lâkûi (*n.*) dinner
kôbe tî midy (*n.phr.*) lunch
kobêla (*n.*) disease
kobêla (*n.*) illness
kobêla sô avunga hîo (*v.phr.*) contagious
kobêla tî simbä (*n.phr.*) motion sickness
koddoro (*n.*) country
koddoro (*n.*) village
koddorosêse (*n.*) republic
kôde tî koddoro (*n.phr.*) country code
kôdesînga (*n.*) dialing code
kofforo (*n.*) locker
kofforo tî datokua (*n.phr.*) postbox
kôgarâ tî wâlï (*n.*) mother-in-law
Kôgbô mbetti-tokua (*n.*) postcard
koiko (*adj.*) single
kôle (*n.*) glue

koli (*n.*) pillow
kôlï (*n.*) husband
kôlï (*n.*) man
kôlï tî zo (*n.*) married man
kôlï-bâgara (*n.*) bull
kôlinngba (*n.*) bull (buffalo)
kombammba (*n.*) single
komblëe (*n.*) suit
kombûka (*v.*) disagree and quit
kombûta (*n.*) computer
kömêresa (*n.*) trade
komeresäa (*n.*) merchant
kommandema (*n.*) authority
kônde (*n.*) account
kônde (na bânge) bank account
kôndo (*n.*) chicken
kôngbâ (*n.*) baggage
kôngbâ (*n.*) luggage
kôngbâ (tî da) (*n.*) furniture
Konndoko (*n.*) spring (season)
konngo (*n.*) plant
konnomi (*n.*) economy
konzalonndo (*n.*) homeless
konzëe (*n.*) holiday
konzëe (*n.*) vacation
kopo (*n.*) cup
kopu (*n.*) jar
kôro (*v.*) across (pierce)
kôro (*v.*) through (pierce)
korrongo piny (*n.*) flat tire
koso (*n.*) pig
kötarä (*n.*) grandfather
kotöon (*n.*) cotton

kotta (*adj.*) big
kotta (*adj.*) main
kotta danzapä (*n.phr.*) cathedral
kotta galâ (*n.phr.*) shopping center
kotta hotto (*n.phr.*) mountain
kotta kpalle (*n.phr.*) disaster
kotta kpalle (*n.phr.*) drama
kotta lêgë (*n.phr.*) highway
kotta magazäni (*n.phr.*) supermarket
kotta matânga (*n.phr.*) festival
kotta nzönî (*adj.phr.*) great
kotta pânde (*n.phr.*) nuts
kotta suimëen (*n.phr.*) bath towel
kotti-wakua (*n.*) assistant
kôya (*n.*) nephew (child of a man's sister)
kôya (*n.*) niece (child of a man's sister)
kôya (*n.*) uncle (mother's brother)
kôzo (*adj.*) first
kôzo kamâ (*n.phr.*) first-class
kôzo na tângo (*adv.phr.*) early
kôzonî (*adv.*) before
kpa (*v.*) look
kpa (*v.*) seem
kpaka-nzerë (*n.*) engraving
kpâkayâo (*n.*) sandals
kpakke (*adj.*) false
kpakkpa (*n.*) bridge
kpâlâ kâmba (*n.*) ribbon
kpâlâ kombûta (*n.*) laptop
kpalando (*n.*) beach
kpalle (*n.*) issue
kpalle (*n.*) problem
kpângi (*n.*) wing

kpângi (*n.*) wing
kpânngbala (*adj.*) flat
kpâsû (*n.*) pen
kpatta (*n.*) dough
kpatta (*n.*) pie
kpâtyâ (*adv.*) drunk
kpë (*v.*) run
kpë na mbârrata (*v.phr.*) ride
kpë zo (*v.phr.*) respect
kpë zo pëpe (*v.phr.*) impolite
kpekpêe (*adj.*) sour
kpëkpesë (*n.*) emergency
kpenngo-zo (*n.*) respect
kpêssere (*adj.*) narrow
kpi (*adj.*) neutral
kpikpîi (*adj.*) sour
kpiti (*n.*) jam
kpîtî (*adv.*) very black
kpo (*v.*) prick
kpo (*prep.*) against
kpo maka (*v.phr.*) limit
kpo na tonga (*v.*) inject
kpo-kekke (*n.*) crutches
kpokkolo (*n.*) wallet
kpön (*n.*) soap
kpön tî pemmbe (*n.phr.*) toothpaste
kpoto (*n.*) hat
kpû (*n.*) rope
kpûdduwen (*n.*) rail
kpûgada (*n.*) train
kpûrû (*n.*) motorcycle
kpûwên (tî lêgë) (*n.phr.*) rail
kredy (*n.*) credit

krêmo (*n.*) cream

kü (*v.*) wait

kü kâpä na (zo) (*v.phr.*) give an appointment to (somebody)

kü tufa (*v.phr.*) bless

kua (*n.*) job

kua (*n.*) use

kua (*n.*) work

kua tî biröo (*n.phr.*) bureaucracy

kuafëre (*n.*) barber

kualî (*n.*) activity

kualî (*n.*) activity

kualî (*n.*) occupation

kuasû (*n.*) secretary

kubû (*n.*) room

kubû tî kpëkpesë (*n.phr.*) emergency room

kubû tî lanngo (*n.phr.*) bedroom

kubû tî tarrango-bongö (*n.phr.*) fitting room

kubû tî tenngo-kôbe (*n.phr.*) dining room

kubû tî tôngbilö (*n.phr.*) conference room

kubû tî wanî (*n.phr.*) private room

kubûlanngo (*n.*) bedroom

kubûlikôlo (*n.*) class

kubû-yamba (*n.*) apartment

kudda (*n.*) debt

kudda (*n.*) loan

kugbë tî kabiny (*n.phr.*) sanitary napkin

kugbë tî kabiny (*n.phr.*) toilet paper

kugbë tî kângbâ (*n.phr.*) aluminum foil

kugbë tî kâsa (*n.phr.*) vegetable

kûi (*v.*) die

kûi na nyonhngo-ngû (*v.phr.*) drown

kükâpä (*n.*) appointment

Kukkuru (*n.*) August
kûkû (*n.*) trap
kukuta (*n.*) layover
kûne (*adj.*) special
kûne gbegô (*n.phr.*) accent
kûngbi (*v.*) break
kuni (*v.*) fix
kuni pa (*v.phr.*) decide
kuni pekô (tî) (*v.phr.*) confirm
kunipa (*n.*) decision
kunndu (*n.*) club
kunndu (*n.*) league
kunngo-kâpä (*n.*) appointment
kunni (*n.*) thigh
kuräan (*n.*) electricity
kuru (*n.*) list
kurulindo (*n.*) directory
kusâra (*n.*) work
kûshi (*n.*) diaper
kûtu (*n.*) knot
kûtu (*n.*) million
kutukutu (*n.*) automobile
kutukutu (*n.*) car
kuturu (*n.*) fig
kwâ (*n.*) death
kwa tî li (*n.phr.*) hair
kwa tî porronyö (*n.phr.*) moustache
kwali (*n.*) hair
kwatäba (*n.*) wool
kwê (*adj.*) all
kwê (*adv.*) entirely
kwê pendere (*adj.phr.*) perfect
kwêzu (*adj.*) general

lâ (*n.*) day
lâ (*n.*) daytime
lâ (*n.*) sun
lâ tî dunngo (*n.phr.*) date of birth
labânge (*n.*) bank
lâdunngo (*n.*) birthday
lâdunngo (*n.*) aniversary
lafâi (*n.*) veil
laggerema (*n.*) rule
lakoppya (*n.*) company
lâkûi (*n.*) evening
lâkwê (*adv.*) always
lalâmba (*n.*) lamp
lâmbâ (*adj.*) thin
lamêre (*n.*) sea
lamonëe (*n.*) change
lando (*n.*) stadium
langi (*n.*) lens
lanngo (*v.*) sleep
lanngo (*n.*) day
lanngo (*v.*) sleep
Lanngo tî Finî Ngû (*n.phr.*) New Year's Day
lapârângba (*n.*) bat (cockroach)
laparra (*n.*) airplane
laparra (*n.*) plane
lâpôso (*n.*) Saturday
larrama (*n.*) army
larramangû (*n.*) navy
lâsô (*n.*) today
lavu (*n.*) honey
lâwa (*pron.*) when
lazwara (*n.*) razor
lê (*n.*) eye

lê (*n.*) face
lê tî kakaö (*n.phr.*) coconut
lê tî kekke (*n.phr.*) fruit
lê tî ngombe (*n.phr.*) bullet
lêbê (*n.*) berry
lêgë (*n.*) road
lêgë âdu daä (*v.phr.*) eventually
lêgë tî gerê (*n.phr.*) path
lêgë tî gerê (*n.phr.*) footpath
lêgë tî sï na (*n.phr.*) access
lêgë tî wên (*n.phr.*) railroad
lêgëdû (*n.*) tunnel
lêgëhurru (*n.*) airline
lêgë-ôko (*adv.*) together
lêgë-ôko (*adj.*) even
leke (*v.*) fix
leke (*v.*) treat
leke pekô tî (*v.phr.*) repair
lêkekke (*n.*) fruit
lêlê (*n.*) kidney
lêmbetti (*n.*) page
lênduzzu (*n.*) weather
lêngbadrâ (*n.*) scene
lêngbi (*n.*) measure
Lengua (*n.*) July
lênngere (*n.*) appendicitis
lenngo (*n.*) administration
lêpêrë (*n.*) cereal
lesöro (*n.*) spring (metal coil)
lesswango (*n.*) rebellion
lêsû (*n.*) letter
lesua (*v.*) rebel
leswa (*n.*) rebellion

---

leswa (*n.*) riot
lêwâ (*n.*) flame
lêyê (*n.*) item
li (*n.*) head
lî (*n.*) act
lî (*n.*) action
lï (*v.*) act
lï (*v.*) admit
lï (*v.*) enter
lï ngû (*v.phr.*) sink
li tî (zo) aturnêe (*v.phr.*) dizzy
li tî da (*n.phr.*) roof
li tî mabôko (*n.phr.*) finger
lida (*n.*) roof
lidöwâ (*n.*) accelerator (gas pedal)
ligbâsû (*n.*) chapter
ligbî (*n.*) source
likângâ (*n.*) peak
likângâ (*n.*) pick (n.)
likpo (*n.*) plug
likunni (*n.*) knee
limo (*n.*) picture
limo-lêgë (*n.*) road map
limondo (*n.*) map
linda (*v.*) join (get in)
lindo (*n.*) address
lîngbi (*v.*) able (be ...)
lîngbi (*v.*) can (modal verb)
lîngbi (*v.*) qualify
lîngbi na (*v.*) fit
lingo na ngangü (*n.phr.*) trespassing
linngbingo (*n.*) fitting
linngo (*n.*) admission

linngo (*adj.*) deep
linngo (*n.*) entrance
linngo (*n.*) entry
liswa (*n.*) stitch
litï (*n.*) finger
lîtri (*n.*) liter
litûtu (*adj.*) equal
litûtu (*adv.*) equally
lîvri (*n.*) pound
lo (*pron.*) he
lo (*pron.*) she
logoma (*v.*) delicious (be ...)
logoma (*v.*) sweet (be ...)
lokôto (*v.*) collect
lökûtu (*n.*) problem
lôlo (*n.*) gold
lonndo (*v.*) leave
lopitäni (*n.*) hospital
lôro (*n.*) gold
lorro (*n.*) hurry
lorro (*n.*) speed
lôso (*n.*) rice
lü (*v.*) bury
lungûla (*v.*) remove
lungûla tenne na li tî (zo) (*v.phr.*) forgive
lurêe (*v.*) wrap
lutti (*v.*) halt
lutti (*v.*) stop

ma (*adv.*) then
mä (*v.*) feel
mä (*v.*) hear
mä (*v.*) listen

mä (*v.*) understand
mä bê (*v.phr.*) believe
mä bê na (*v.phr.*) trust
mabôko (*n.*) hand
mabôko-vurü (*n.*) innocent
madäma (*n.*) lady
mafüta (*n.*) fat
mafüta (*n.*) oil
magazäni (*n.*) shop
magazäni (*n.*) store
maimâi (*n.*) drug
maka (*n.*) border
maka (*n.*) limit
makâko (*n.*) monkey
makala (*n.*) cake
makalanngo (*n.*) deadline
maka-lorro (*n.*) speed limit
makongö (*n.*) virus
makorony (*n.*) noodles
makorony (*n.*) pasta
mamâ (*n.*) mother
mamândya (*n.*) constitution
mamâ-tunnge (*n.*) tutor
mamêre (*n.*) nun
mamîwatta (*n.*) siren
mä-na-bê (*n.*) Protestant
manda (*v.*) learn
manda (*v.*) study
mângbi (*n.*) agreement
mangbonnga (*n.*) trunk
manngbingo (*n.*) agreement
manngbingo-terê kpâkpu (*n.phr.*) compromise
manngo-bê (*n.*) trust

manngo-terê nzönî pëpe (*n.phr.*) misunderstanding
mâpa (*n.*) bread
mâpa (*n.*) loaf
mâpa-na-kâsa (*n.*) sandwich
marä (*n.*) kind
marä (*n.*) tribe
marä (*n.*) type
marä tî mênë (*n.phr.*) blood type
maräbongö (*n.*) uniform
mârâke (*n.*) score (n.)
marakêe (*v.*) score (v.)
marä-nginza (*n.*) currency
maseka (*n.*) young
maseka (*n.*) youth
maseka-kôlï (*n.*) boy
maseka-wâlï (*n.*) girl
masïni (*n.*) engine
masïni (*n.*) machine
masïni tî sukkulango-bongö (*n.phr.*) washing machine
masïni tî sukûla na kurru nî (*n.phr.*) dry cleaner
masïni-petesû (*n.*) printer
masïni-pette (*n.*) press
masûa (*n.*) boat
masûa (*n.*) ship
maswar tî ngbondâ tî bebë (*n.phr.*) baby wipes
mataläa (*n.*) mattress
matânga (*n.*) party
Mâti (*n.*) math
mazende (*n.*) vanilla
mba masûa (*v.phr.*) sail
mbâgë (*n.*) piece
mbâgë (*n.*) side
mbâgë bata-yamba (*n.phr.*) spare part

mbäli (*n.*) size
mbäli tî sannzengo-nginza (*n.phr.*) exchange rate
mbamba (*n.*) lime (mineral)
mbanngo-ngö (*n.phr.*) navigation
mbanza-X (*n.*) x-ray
mbârrata (*n.*) horse
mbâssambala (*num.*) seven
mbatê (*n.*) regime (eating)
mbatta (*n.*) saddle
mbattana (*n.*) base
mbattana (*n.*) basement
mbattana (*n.*) dock
mbattana (*n.*) platform
mbella (*n.*) directions
mbella (*n.*) order (instruction)
mbembe (*n.*) clock
mbembe (*n.*) watch
mbênî (*adv.*) again
mbênî (*adj.*) extra
mbênî (*adv.*) more
mbênî (*adj.*) some
mbênî (...) kirîkiri (*n.phr.*) any
mbênî ndê (*adj.phr.*) other
mbênî yê (*n.phr.*) something
mbênî zo (*n.phr.*) someone
mbere (*n.*) contract
mberêka (*n.*) kettle
mbeto (*v.*) fear
mbetti (*n.*) letter
mbetti (*n.*) paper
mbetti kö-na-ngö (*n.phr.*) boarding pass
mbettidungo (*n.*) birth certificate
mbettifûta (*n.*) bill

mbettikâpä (*n.*) calendar
mbettilêgë tî gue-mo-gä (*n.phr.*) round-trip ticket
mbetti-sango (*n.*) newspaper
mbettisînga (*n.*) e-mail
mbetti-tokua (*n.*) mail
mbettiyinda (*n.*) guidebook
mbetti-yindä (*n.*) guidebook
mbï (*pron.*) I
mbï (*pron.*) me
mbîndä (*n.*) fog
mbipa (*n.*) pigeon
mbîrrimbiri (*adj.*) correct
mbîrrimbiri (*adj.*) right
mbo (*n.*) dog
mbö (*n.*) gas
mbö (*n.*) air
mboma (*n.*) almond
mbongo (*n.*) south
mbôo (*v.*) wipe
mbrâmbrâ (*n.*) seven
mbupa (*n.*) word
mburuwâ (*n.*) ash
mbuttu (*n.*) sand
me (*conj.*) but
me (*n.*) breast
me (*v.*) climb
mê (*n.*) ear
meambe (*n.*) eight
meka na lê (*v.phr.*) estimate
mêkê (asï ...) (*adv.*) full
mekka (*n.*) note
melanzêe (*v.*) mix
mene (*v.*) swallow

mênë (*n.*) blood
menngawâ (*n.*) flame
menngbo (*n.*) glue
mêtere (*n.*) meter
mêzä (*n.*) desk
mêzä (*n.*) table
mêzä tî gbelêda (*n.*) front desk
mêzä-sango (*n.*) information desk
mezû (*n.*) lift
mezû (*n.*) elevator
mikkorônde (*n.*) microwave
mîngi (*adj.*) many
mîngi (*adv.*) much
mîngi (*adv.*) a lot
mîngi (*adv.*) very
mîngi nî (*adv.phr.*) most of the time
mîngi tî (*adj.phr.*) the majority of
mizilïmi (*n.*) Muslim
mo (*pron.*) you (singular)
modô (*n.*) young
môlengê (*n.*) child
môlengê (*n.*) kid
môlengê tî (zo) tî kôlï (*n.phr.*) son
môlengê tî (zo) tî wâlï (*n.phr.*) daughter
môlengê-kôlï (*n.*) boy
môlengê-kôlï tî (zo) (*n.phr.*) son
môlengê-wâlï (*n.*) girl
môlengê-wâlï tî(zo) (*n.phr.*) daughter
molongö (*n.*) queue
môndoro (*n.*) watch
mopêre (*n.*) priest
mosokëe (*n.*) mosque
mosoro (*n.*) fortune

motarâka (*n.*) menu
motöro (*n.*) engine
motöro (*n.*) motor
mozoko (*n.*) music
Msk. (*n.*) Ms. (title)
mû (*v.*) take
mü (*v.*) cure
mû mabôko (*v.phr.*) aid
mû mabôko na (*v.phr.*) help
mû mabôko na (*v.phr.*) assist
mû na (*v.*) give
mû ngû (*v.phr.*) sink
mû paradôo na (*v.phr.*) pardon
mû pekô nî (*v.phr.*) follow (it)
mû pekô tî (*v.phr.*) follow (+complement)
mû terê na (*v.phr.*) marry
mû zêndo na (*v.phr.*) promise
muen (*adj.*) smooth
munna (*n.*) load
munngo na (*n.*) giving to
munngo na (*n.*) delivery
munngo-fotöo na zanngo wâ (*n.*) flash photography
munngo-mabôko (*n.*) aid
munngo-mabôko (*n.*) rescue
munngo-terê (*n.*) marriage
munngo-terê (*n.*) wedding
munngo-yorö (*n.*) medication
munngo-zo na nzï nî (*n.*) kidnap
Mvuka (*n.*) September

na (*prep.*) and
na bï sô (*n.phr.*) tonight
na donngo-terê (*n.phr.*) zealous

na gbe tî *(prep.)* below
na gbe tî *(prep.)* under
na gbenî *(adv.phr.)* low
na gbenî *(adv.)* down
na gîgî *(n.phr.)* outdoor
na gîgî *(n.phr.)* out
na kobêla *(n.phr.)* sick
na lanngo na lê *(n.phr.)* drowsy
na lêgë nî *(adv.phr.)* normally
na lêgë nî äpe *(n.phr.)* wrong
na lêgë tî ndya *(n.phr.)* legal
na lêgë tî ndya *(n.phr.)* official
na lêgë tî ndya pëpe *(n.phr.)* illegal
na lorro *(adv.phr.)* rapidly
na ndën *(n.phr.)* early (in the morning)
na ndo kwê *(n.phr.)* anywhere
na ndo ôko äpe *(n.phr.)* not at one place
na ndo ôko äpe *(n.phr.)* nowhere
na ndö tî *(prep.phr.)* on
na ndö tî *(n.phr.)* concerning
na ndö tî kua *(n.phr.)* busy
na ndo wa *(n.phr.)* where
na ndöbê tî *(n.phr.)* over
na ndönî *(adv.)* above
na nduzzu *(n.phr.)* loud
na nduzzu *(n.phr.)* up
na ngonzo *(n.phr.)* angry
na nzara *(n.phr.)* hungry
na nzara tî ngû *(n.phr.)* thirsty
na nzerekâsa daä *(n.phr.)* spicy
na pâsi na bê *(n.phr.)* sad
na pekô *(n.phr.)* after
na pekô *(n.phr.)* later

na pekô tângo (*n.phr.*) late
na pekô tî (*prep.phr.*) behind
na poppo tî (*prep.*) among
na sêngê bongö (*n.phr.*) casual
na sîrriri (*adv.phr.*) safe
na terê tî (*prep.*) against
na yânî (*adv.phr.*) inside
Nabanndüru (*n.*) November
nanäa (*n.*) mint
ndâ (*n.*) end
ndâ (*n.*) purpose
ndâ (*n.*) reason
ndâgobo (*n.*) wrist
ndâlêgë tî bîsi (*n.phr.*) bus terminal
ndâmbo (*adj.*) half
ndângbâ kêtê nî (*n.phr.*) minimum
ndanndara (*n.*) fog
ndäpêrê (*n.*) morning
ndäpêrrere (*n.*) morning
ndarä (*n.*) wisdom
ndätu (*n.*) dawn
ndaû (*n.*) accident
ndê (*adj.*) different
ndê (*adj.*) sacred
ndê mîngi (*adj.phr.*) unusual
ndeko (*n.*) girlfriend
ndeko (*n.*) boyfriend
ndembë (*n.*) instant
ndembë (*n.*) moment
ndembö (*n.*) rubber
ndembö tî gerê (*n.*) football (soccer)
ndembö tî gerê (*n.*) soccer
ndembö tî sakpä (*n.*) basketball

ndimâ (*n.*) mystery
ndîmon (*n.*) orange
ndo (*n.*) location
ndo (*n.*) place
ndo angbâ sêngê (*n.phr.*) vacancy
ndo tî lanngo (*n.phr.*) accommodation
ndo tî ngyângunu (*n.phr.*) gym
ndo tî sukkulango-bongö (*n.*) laundromat
ndo tî sukkulango-bongö (*n.phr.*) laundry
ndöbê (*n.*) cover
ndöbê (*n.*) top
ndofô (*adj.*) comfortable
ndofono (*n.*) park
ndoggo (*n.*) amount
ndoggo (*n.*) price
ndokko (*n.*) flower
ndokpê (*n.*) refuge
ndölê (*n.*) forehead
ndombe (*n.*) shopkeeper
ndo-mokondô (*n.*) sanctuary
ndôngô (*n.*) pepper
ndongoro (*n.*) neighborhood
Ndorobugbë (*n.*) autumn
ndoto (*n.*) level
ndotti (*n.*) shoulder
ndowâ (*n.*) heat
ndöyê (*n.*) love
ndû (*v.*) touch
ndûmbu (*adj.*) naked
ndurü (*adj.*) short
ndurü (*adj.*) ready
ndurü ge (*adv.phr.*) nearby
ndurü na (*adj.phr.*) near to

ndurü na *(adj.phr.)* next to
nduttu *(n.)* pot
nduzzu *(n.)* sky
ndya *(n.)* law
ndya ake *(v.phr.)* prohibit
ndyayângâ *(n.)* grammar
nenêe *(adj.)* heavy
nenga *(v.)* weigh
nêzi *(n.)* snow
ngâ *(adv.)* also
ngâakô *(n.)* sugar cane
ngâakô *(n.)* sugar cane
ngäbiö *(n.)* arthritis
ngandä *(n.)* hailstone
ngandängombe *(n.)* bullet
nganga wasurrungo-zo *(n.phr.)* surgeon
nganga-pemmbe *(n.)* dentist
ngangatyen *(n.)* dentist
ngangü *(adj.)* hard
ngangü *(adj.)* sensitive
ngangü sonngo li *(n.phr.)* migraine
ngarangâra *(n.)* ladder
ngarangâra *(n.)* stairs
ngarangâra tî masïni *(n.)* escalator
ngäsa *(n.)* goat
ngbâ *(v.)* stay
ngbadrâ *(n.)* theater
ngbanga *(n.)* reason
ngbanga *(n.)* trial
ngbanga tî *(n.phr.)* because of
ngbanga tî nye *(n.phr.)* why
ngbangatî *(conj.)* for fear (of/to)
ngbangbo *(n.)* cent

ngbangbo (*n.*) hundred
ngbasandaû (*n.*) insurance
ngbasandaû tî sênî (*n.*) health insurance
ngbengë tî mozoko (*n.*) musical instrument
ngbengëkpê (*n.*) vehicle
ngbennda (*n.*) bottle
ngbennda tî sêse (*n.*) jug
ngbenngewe (*n.*) coin
ngbêre (*adj.*) old
Ngberere (*n.*) October
ngbö (*n.*) snake
ngbôn (*adj.*) brown
ngbondâ (*n.*) rear
ngbonga (*n.*) bell
ngbonga (*n.*) hour
ngembö (*n.*) activist
ngendë (*n.*) chair
ngendë-gbâzâ (*n.*) wheelchair
ngêrë (*n.*) cost
ngêrë (*n.*) price
ngêrë (*n.*) prize
ngêrë aso (*v.phr.*) expensive
ngêrë tî kubû (*n.phr.*) room rate
ngêrêngö (*n.*) ring (sound)
nginza (*n.*) money
nginza (*n.*) silver
nginza tî koddoro-wandê (*n.*) foreign currency
nginza tî kua (*n.phr.*) income
nginza tî luemäa (*n.phr.*) rent
ngö (*n.*) corner
ngoangoa (*n.*) seed
ngoi (*n.*) period
ngoi (*n.*) season

ngoindya (*n.*) legislature
ngombe (*n.*) gun
ngonda (*n.*) jungle
ngonngo (*n.*) corner
ngötâ (*n.*) triangle
ngû (*n.*) age
ngû (*n.*) liquid
ngû (*n.*) river
ngû (*n.*) water
ngû (*n.*) year
ngû balë-ôko (*n.phr.*) decade
ngû tî kâsa (*n.phr.*) sauce
ngû tî kôzo (*n.phr.*) last year
ngû tî lêkâsa (*n.*) juice
ngû tî pekô (*n.phr.*) next year
Ngubë (*n.*) April
ngûkâsa (*n.*) soup
ngûli (*n.*) liquor
ngûmbâ (*n.*) rate (anatomy)
ngûmbetti (*n.*) ink
ngûme (*n.*) milk
ngungu (*n.*) fly (insect)
ngungu (*n.*) mosquito
ngunu (*n.*) energy
ngunu (*n.*) power
ngunuhalëzo (*n.*) democracy
ngunzä (*n.*) cassava leaf
ngunzä (*adj.*) green
ngûnzapä (*n.*) rain
ngûnzapä (*n.*) rain
ngura (*n.*) right (owed)
ngurrungo (*n.*) detour
nguru (*v.*) around

ngurugbya (*n.*) government
ngûrûngbi (*adj.*) complicated (be ...)
nguzü (*n.*) worm
ngyâ (*n.*) comedy
ngyâ (*n.*) entertainment
ngyâ (*n.*) fun
ngyâ (*n.*) game
ngyâ (*n.*) play
ngyângunu (*n.*) sport
nî (*pron.*) it
nîgïsi (*num.*) zero
nilöon (*n.*) plastic
nngbondö lenge (*n.phr.*) jewelry
nommoro (*n.*) number
nommoro tî datokua (*n.phr.*) postal code
nommoro tî hurru (*n.phr.*) flight number
nommoro tî kitî (*n.phr.*) seat number
nommoro tî sînga (*n.phr.*) phone number
nyama (*n.*) animal
nyama (*n.*) meat
nyama tî koddoro (*n.phr.*) pet
nyama tî koso (*n.phr.*) pork
nyama tî lamêre (*n.phr.*) seafood
nyama tî yorrongo (*n.phr.*) steak
nyamma (*n.*) wide wild landscape
nyammakuru (*n.*) desert
nyammangû (*n.*) ocean
nyammangû (*n.*) ocean
nyammasêse (*n.*) continent
nyâö (*n.*) cat
nye (*pron.*) what
Nyenye (*n.*) January
nyîmbâ (*n.*) member

nyîtäba (*n.*) lamb
nyön (*v.*) drink
nyonhngo (*n.*) beverage
nyonhngo (*n.*) drink
nyonhngo-mânga (*n.*) smoking
nyötûngu (*n.*) harbor
nzapä (*n.*) religion
nze (*n.*) month
nze (*n.*) moon
nzêen (*v.*) tire
nzeenngo terê (*n.*) disability
nzêkkede (*n.*) insect
nzerekâsa (*n.*) seasoning
nzerrengo (*n.*) flavor
nzerrengo (*adj.*) pleasant
nzerrengo (*n.*) taste
nzerrengo yângâ (*n.*) appetite
nzï (*n.*) concussion
nzï (*n.*) fraud
nzï (*n.*) rob
nzï (*v.*) steal
nzï-mo-kpë (*n.*) shoplifting
nzîna ngbonga (*n.phr.*) minute
nzö (*n.*) corn
nzönî (*adj.*) good
nzönî alîngbi (*adj.phr.*) fare
nzönî dutï (*n.phr.*) amenities
nzönî! (*interj.*) OK
nzoô (*adj.*) free
nzorôko (*n.*) color
nzöyê (*n.*) goods
nzü (*n.*) fly (insect)

ôke (*adj.*) how much
ôke (*adv.*) how many
ôko (*adj.*) alone
ôko (*n.*) one
ôko (*adj.*) same
ôko äpe (*adv.phr.*) never
ôko ôko (*adj.phr.*) every
okü (*n.*) five
omanä (*n.*) six
omenë (*n.*) six
otâ (*n.*) three
otâzi (*n.*) hostage
otêle (*n.*) hotel
ötêle (*n.*) altar

pa (*n.*) word
pafûe (*n.*) poem
pafungûla (*n.*) password
pakara (*n.*) sir
paläa (*n.*) tray
palâzi (*n.*) beach
palî (*n.*) v.
palüh (*n.*) flu
palüh (*n.*) influenza
pandara (*n.*) youth
pande (*n.*) sentence
pânde (*n.*) point
panzêe (*v.*) worry
papa (*v.*) dispute
papa (*n.*) spoon
paradôo (*n.*) pardon
paradôo (*n.*) sorry
parra (*n.*) egg

pâsi (*n.*) pain
pâsi na bê (*n.*) worry
passapôro (*n.*) passport
passema (*n.*) event
patalöon (*n.*) pants
patröon (*n.*) employer
payinnda (*n.*) directions
pedäle (*n.*) pedal
pedalëe tî ammbreâzi (*n.*) clutch pedal
pekô (*n.*) back
pekô (*n.*) rear
pekô tî bêkombïte (*n.phr.*) afternoon
pekôyyanga tî nzêkkede (*n.phr.*) insect bite
pelêma (*n.*) tag
pelengû (*n.*) profile
pemmbe (*n.*) tooth
pemmbe tî vïtêsi (*n.phr.*) gear
pendâ (*n.*) influence
pendere (*adj.*) beautiful
pendere (*adj.*) nice
penzepa (*n.*) phrase
pepe (*n.*) pipe
pepesisâ (*n.*) vein
pêrë (*n.*) grass
pêrë (*n.*) herb
peremisïon (*n.*) permission
peremy (*n.*) license
peremy (*n.*) permit
peremy tî (gbottongo-) kutukutu (*n.phr.*) driver's license
pese (*n.*) sex
pete gôro (*v.phr.*) bribe
peteta (*n.*) pottery
petröle (*n.*) petrol

pezêe (v.) weigh
piabattango (n.) reservation
piagbarra (n.) schedule
pialö (n.) project
pialökua (n.) program
pîka (v.) knock
pîka (v.) shoot
pîka (n.) shot
pîka (v.) type
pîka na kä (v.phr.) hurt
pîka pïpï (v.phr.) toll
pîka sâko (v.phr.) clap
pîka sînga (v.phr.) dial
pikkango-bê (n.) pulse
pilîli (n.) pill
pilovëre (n.) pull
pinality (n.) penalty
pinîi (v.) punish
pinningo (n.) sanction
pinningo (ngyângunu) (n.) penalty
piny (n.) tire
pïpï (n.) toll
pîri (adj.) pure
pïsîni (n.) pool
Pkr. (n.) Mr. (title)
polêlê (adj.) public
polï (n.) compensation
polîsi (n.) police
pômbe (n.) pump
pômo (n.) apple
pôon (n.) bridge
pôon (n.) deck
popôto (n.) mud

popôto (*n.*) pudding
porosö (*n.*) politics
porro (*n.*) leather
porro (*n.*) shoe
porro (*n.*) skin
porronyo (*n.*) lip
pôsö tî Finî Ngû (*n.phr.*) New Year's Eve
potopôto (*n.*) mud
Potto (*n.*) Europe
pozzonengo-kôbe (*n.*) food poisoning
prezidäan (*n.*) president
pumbä tî kwâ (*n.phr.*) funeral
pupu (*n.*) air
pupu (*n.*) wind
puse (*adj.*) public
pûsu (*v.*) push
pusupûsu (*n.*) cart

qündâ (*n.*) basement

radïo (*n.*) radio
râmba (*n.*) ramp
rasïo (*n.*) ratio
resy (*n.*) receipt
retêe (*v.*) arrest
rettengo (*n.*) arrest
rezëen (*n.*) grape
ridöo (*n.*) veil
rîski (*n.*) risk
robinëe (*n.*) faucet

sa (*v.*) throw
sa mbeto (*v.phr.*) scare

sa mênë (*v.phr.*) bleed
sa ngonzo (*v.phr.*) irritate
sa ngû (*v.phr.*) swim
sâa-lorro (*n.*) speedometer
sade (*n.*) muscle
sagbê (*n.*) organ
saggba (*n.*) advertisement
sâi (*n.*) tea
sâkadö (*n.*) backpack
sâki (*num.*) thousand
sakî (*n.*) virus
sâkigarâmo (*n.*) kilogram
sâkimêtere (*n.*) kilometer
sakka (*n.*) yeast
sakpä (*n.*) basket
sakpä tî galâ (*n.phr.*) shopping basket
sakpä tî pekô (*n.phr.*) knapsack
sakpäbî (*n.*) trash
sâla (*v.*) do
saläde (*n.*) lettuce
saläde (*n.*) salad
sambêla (*v.*) pray
Sambuse (*adj.*) neutral
sân (*prep.*) without
sân kamenne (*n.phr.*) rude
sân kiri (*n.phr.*) duty-free
sandûku (*n.*) box
sandûku (*n.*) suitcase
sangbi (*n.*) intersection
sango (*n.*) information
sango (*n.*) news
sanna (*n.*) torture
sanna (*n.*) violence

sanngo ngû (*n.phr.*) spring (water)
sannzengo marä-nginza (*n.*) currency exchange
sannzo (*n.*) infection
sanzêe (*v.*) change
sanzêe (*v.*) exchange
sanzêe (*v.*) replace
sara (*v.*) itch
sâra (*v.*) act
sâra (*v.*) do
sâra (*v.*) make
sâra (*v.*) treat
sâra kua (*v.phr.*) work
sâra kusâra (*v.phr.*) work
sâra mayëre (*v.phr.*) trick
sâra mbeto (*v.phr.*) afraid (be ...)
sâra na (*v.*) use
sâra ngyâ (*v.phr.*) play
sâra syonî na (*v.phr.*) harm
sarala (*n.*) umbrella
saratëe (*n.*) dirt
saratëe (*adj.*) dirty
saravêe (*v.*) serve
saravêe-terê (*n.*) self-service
saravëte (*n.*) napkin
sarawîsi (*n.*) service
sarawîsi tî kubû (*n.phr.*) room service
sarrazema (*n.*) charge
sasa (*n.*) diarrhea
sattelîti (*n.*) satellite
savâa (*v.*) cure
savôon (*n.*) soap
savôon tî kyonngo-kwâ (*n.*) shaving cream
Sêboro (*n.*) quality

sêdêe (*n.*) CD
sêgbya (*n.*) royalty
sêku (*n.*) century
sêkü (*adj.*) permanent
sêkü (*adj.*) secular
sêlêgë (*n.*) itinerary
sêlêgë (*n.*) route
selêka (*n.*) marriage
sêlêngbandrâ (*n.*) scenery
sêlorro (*n.*) speed
sembê (*n.*) plate
sembë (*n.*) dish
sêmenngo (*n.*) altitude
seminëre (*n.*) seminar
senäa (*n.*) senate
senatëre (*n.*) senator
sêndâmasïni (*n.*) mechanic
sêndowâ (*n.*) temperature
sênduzu (*n.*) climate
sêngê (*adj.*) free
sêngê (*adj.*) ordinary
sêngê (*adj.*) standard
sênî (*n.*) health
sênndamâti (*n.*) math
sênndaye (*n.*) science
sennde (*n.*) cemetery
sennde (*n.*) sculpture
senngbingo (*n.*) settlement
sênôn ôko (*n.phr.*) one-way
sêpê (*adj.*) sharp
sêpelle (*adj.*) thin
serêe (*v.*) restrict
serrengo (*adj.*) narrow

sêse (*n.*) earth
sêse (*n.*) floor
sêse (*n.*) ground
sêse (*n.*) land
sêse (*n.*) territory
sêse ayêngi (*v.phr.*) earthquake
sêse tî kândo (*n.phr.*) campground
sesêe (*adj.*) bitter
sêsewwa (*n.*) relationship
sêtângbi (*n.*) relationship
sewwa (*n.*) relative
sewwa (*n.*) parent
sewwa (*n.*) family
sewwa (*n.*) relative
seyä (*n.*) babysitter
seyä (*n.*) nurse
sêyângbangbo (*n.*) percentage
sêyê tî wanî (*n.phr.*) privacy
shampwen (*n.*) shampoo
shaynngo (*n.*) breakfast
shokoläa (*n.*) chocolate
sï (*v.*) arrive
sï (*v.*) fill
sidäa (*n.*) AIDS
sigarëti (*n.*) cigarette
siggingo (*n.*) exit
sïgî (*n.*) exit
sîi (*n.*) saw
simäan (*n.*) cement
simba (*v.*) travel
simbä (*n.*) travel
simmba (*n.*) hike
sindimäa (*n.*) cinema

sindimäa (*n.*) film
sînga (*n.*) phone
sînga (*n.*) telephone
sînga puse (*n.phr.*) public telephone
sînga tî bozö (*n.phr.*) mobile phone
sînga tî bozö (*n.*) portable
sîngasûkô (*n.*) fax
singïla (*n.*) thank you
sinimäa (*n.*) cinema
sinimäa (*n.*) film
sinnagôgo (*n.*) synagogue
sinngo (*n.*) arrival
sira (*v.*) deny
sirä (*n.*) denial
siri (*n.*) lice
siröo tî tîkö (*n.phr.*) cough syrup
sîrriri (*n.*) peace
sîrriri (*adj.*) quiet
sisâ (*n.*) nerve
sissitêma (*n.*) system
sïvîli (*n.*) civilian
sizöo (*n.*) scissors
sô (*adj.*) that
sô (*adj.*) that
sô (*adj.*) this
sö (*v.*) save
sô a bata (*v.phr.*) spare
sô a fûta awe (*v.phr.*) paid
sô a kä awe (*v.phr.*) sold
sô a mû na (*v.phr.*) furnished
sô a nzï awe (*v.phr.*) stolen
sô agirisa (*v.phr.*) lost
sô ahôle na dê awe (*v.phr.*) frozen

sô akânga (*v.phr.*) close
sô akânga (*prep.*) closed
sô amë ngo / mama tî ngo (*prep.*) pregnant
sô angbâ (*v.phr.*) left
sô angbâ môlengê (*v.phr.*) minor
sô angbâ sêngê (*v.phr.*) vacant
sô awara sannzo (*v.phr.*) infected
sô ayeke na lêgë nî pëpe (*prep.*) incorrect
sô ayolia (*v.phr.*) melt
sö benda (*v.phr.*) win
sô ge (*adj.phr.*) this
sô kâ (*adj.phr.*) that
sô warrango-nî ngangü (*v.phr.*) rare
sô zo alîngbi tî zîa bê daä (*v.phr.*) reliable
sonngo (*adj.*) sore
sonngo li (*n.phr.*) headache
sonngo li (*n.phr.*) fever
sonngo mê (*n.*) earache
sonngo pemmbe (*n.*) toothache
sonngo terê (*n.*) sore
soro (*v.*) select
soro (*v.*) vote
soroka (*v.*) ration (v.)
sorroka (*n.*) ration (n.)
sorrongo (*n.*) option
sorrongo (*n.*) selection
sosêti (*n.*) socket
sosêti (*n.*) condom
sosêti (*n.*) sock
sosisöon (*n.*) sausage
sozyaa (*n.*) soy
su (*v.*) suck
sû (*v.*) write

sû pekô (*v.*) copy
suali (*n.*) comb
suimëen (*n.*) towel
sukâni (*n.*) sugar
sûkere (*n.*) sugar
sûkkpuru-sukkpuru (*adv.*) uncomfortable
sukkulango-ngû (*n.*) bath
sukkulango-ngû (*n.*) shower
sukkungo (*adj.*) swelling
sukkungo ngû (*n.phr.*) flood
sûkô (*n.*) copy
sukûla (*v.*) wash
sukûla ngû (*v.*) bathe
sûnga (*v.*) record
sunngango (*n.*) registration
sunngo-mbella (*n.*) prescription
sunngo-yângâ (*n.*) kiss
surä (*n.*) section
surrungo-zo (*n.*) surgery
sûru (*v.*) rip
susu (*n.*) fish
sûsûka (*prep.*) until
swa (*n.*) needle
syonî (*adj.*) bad
syonî (*n.*) danger
syonngahözo (*n.*) AIDS
syonngahözo (*n.*) HIV
syonngan (*n.*) pest

taâ (*adj.*) true
taâ-tenne (*n.*) truth
täba (*n.*) sheep
tabî (*n.*) trash

tâbolo (*n.*) table
takasîi (*n.*) taxi
takisîi (*n.*) taxi
talâtu (*n.*) television
tälitï (*n.*) thumb
tambûla (*v.*) walk
tambûla (*n.*) walk
tândâ (*n.*) tent
tângo (*n.*) time
tângömbo (*n.*) sterile woman
tanngbingo (*n.*) junction
täpandë (*n.*) example
täpandë (*n.*) sample
tapöon (*n.*) tampon
tapy (*n.*) carpet
tapy (*n.*) rug
tara (*v.*) try
tarä (*n.*) grandfather
tarä (*n.*) grandmother
tarakwâ (*n.*) risk
tara-mo-bâa (*n.*) experience
taratarra (*n.*) glass
taratarra (*n.*) glasses (eye)
taratarra (*n.*) mirror
taratarra tî lê (*n.*) eyeglasses
tarra (*n.*) test
târrara (*adj.*) pure
tâsôkö (*n.*) oxygen
tatarra (*n.*) glasses (eye)
tatarra (*n.*) mirror
tawâ (*n.*) pan
te (*v.*) bite
te (*v.*) eat

te kôbe tî lâkûi (*v.phr.*) dine
te yâ tî (*v.phr.*) chew
tekugbë (*n.*) vegetarian
têmbere (*n.*) stamp
têmë (*n.*) rock
têmë (*n.*) stone
tene (*v.*) say
tene (*v.*) speak
tene (*v.*) tell
tênë (*n.*) stone
tene mvene (*v.phr.*) lie
tene tenne (*v.phr.*) talk
tene tenne (*v.phr.*) express
têngbi (*v.*) join
têngbi (*v.*) meet
tenne (*n.*) talk (n.)
tenne (*n.*) issue
tenngo (*n.*) eating
tenngo (*n.*) profit
terê (*n.*) body
tere (*n.*) spider
terro (*n.*) terrorist
tê-yâ-fono (*n.*) picnic
tî (*prep.*) of
tï (*v.*) fall
tî (*prep.*) about
tî Afrîka (*n.phr.*) African (*adj.*)
tî Amerîka (*n.phr.*) American (*adj.*)
tî bingo-nî (*n.phr.*) disposable
tî bolingo (*n.phr.*) romantic
tî boro zo (*n.phr.*) human
tî dadä (*n.phr.*) electric
tî derêe (*n.phr.*) mural

tî ë (*n.phr.*) our
tî fadësô (*n.phr.*) actual
tî gbenî (*n.phr.*) underneath side
tî gîgî (*n.phr.*) outdoors side
tî gira (*n.phr.*) folk
tî gira (*n.phr.*) traditional
tï gôh (*v.phr.*) accurate (be ...)
tï gôh (*v.phr.*) exact (be ...
tî kambagä nî (*n.phr.*) mandatory
tî kêtê ngêrë (*n.phr.*) cheap
tî kêtê ngêrë (*n.phr.*) inexpensive
tî kêtê nî (*n.phr.*) minor
tî kêtê tângo (*n.phr.*) temporary
tî kobêla tî makâko (*n.phr.*) epileptic
tî koddoro (*n.phr.*) traditional
tî kôlï na wâlï (*n.phr.*) marital
tî kôlï na wâlï (*n.phr.*) heterosexual
tî konnongo lê (*n.phr.*) large
tî kôzo (*n.phr.*) last
tî kpâa nî (*n.phr.*) original
tî kpenngo-zo (*n.phr.*) polite
tî kûi terê (*v.phr.*) anesthetic
tî kuräan (*n.phr.*) electric
tî lâkwê (*n.phr.*) ever
tî larrama (*n.phr.*) military
tî lêgë nî (*adj.phr.*) proper
tî lêgë nî (*n.phr.*) regular
tî lênî (*n.*) actual
tî li (*n.phr.*) mental
tî marä (*n.phr.*) ethnic
tî marä nî (*n.phr.*) category-specific
tî marä nî (*n.phr.*) categorial
tî maräzo (*n.phr.*) ethnic

tî mbeto (*n.phr.*) scary
tî mbï (*n.phr.*) mine
tî mîngi nî (*n.phr.*) most of the time
tî mîtâ wanî (*n.phr.*) intimate
tî ndarä (*n.phr.*) wise
tî ndo nî (*n.phr.*) local
tî ndya (*n.phr.*) legal
tî ngbêre ndo (*n.phr.*) antique
tî ngoi (*n.phr.*) seasonal
tî ngû ôko (*n.phr.*) for one year
tî ngû ôko ôko (*n.phr.*) annual
tî ngyâ (*n.phr.*) funny
tî nyamma (*n.phr.*) wild
tî passa (*n.phr.*) lucky
tî pekô (*n.phr.*) next
tî poppokodoro (*n.phr.*) international
tî pumbä (*n.phr.*) ceremonial
tî pumbä (*n.phr.*) formal
tî sagbê (*n.phr.*) organic
tî sênndami (*adj.*) chemical
tî taâ-tenne (*adj.*) serious
tî tökêtê nî (*adv.phr.*) at least
tî tokkota nî (*adv.phr.*) the upmost
tî wakodëkua (*adj.*) professional
tî wanî (*adj.*) personal
tî wanî (*adj.*) private
tî wato (*n.phr.*) hostile
tî yâda (*n.*) indoor
tî yângâ (*n.phr.*) oral
tî yângbö (*n.phr.*) domestic
tî zêggbelemi (*n.phr.*) nuclear
tî zo ôko (*n.phr.*) individual
tîa (*v.*) miss (be missing)

tîa mênë (*v.phr.*) anemic
tikëe (*n.*) ticket
tikëe tî kêsi (*n.*) sales receipt
tîkö (*n.*) cough
tiri (*n.*) battle
tirwäar (*n.*) drawer
tîsa (*v.*) invite
tiyöo (*n.*) pipe
to (*v.*) send
tö (*n.*) main
tö (*n.*) east
to (na) sîngasûkô (*v.phr.*) fax
tö kôbe (*v.phr.*) cook
to mbetti (*v.phr.*) mail
tö ndânî (*v.phr.*) start
tö tî (*v.phr.*) step to
tô tô tô (*adv.*) non stop
tô tô tô (*adv.*) fluently
tökêtê (*adj.*) minimum
tokka (*n.*) scar
tokkota (*adj.*) maximum
tokkwango-yê na datokua (*n.phr.*) postage
tokua (*n.*) commission
tokua (*n.*) massage
tokua (*v.*) send
tomâte (*n.*) tomato
tomba-nzêkkede (*n.*) insect repellant
tömokönzi (*n.*) president
tondo (*v.*) report
töndombe (*n.*) manager
töngana (*conj.*) if
töngana kwâ (*adv.phr.*) unconscious
töngana nye (*adv.*) how

tôngbi (*n.*) communication
tôngbilö (*n.*) conference
tôngömbo (*n.*) sterile man
tôngömbo (*n.*) sterile man
tonngo ndâ tî (*n.phr.*) beginning of
tonngo-ndânî (*n.*) beginning
tonngo-yê bîakü lo-ôko (*n.phr.*) automatic transmission
tôo kôbe (*v.phr.*) cook
toronga (*n.*) syringe
torôrô (*adv.*) fluently
torôrô (*adv.*) straight
toto (*v.*) cry
toto (*n.*) noise
toto (*v.*) ring
toto (*n.*) sound
töwakûku (*n.*) chef
trëen (*n.*) train
triköo (*n.*) knit
trolëe (*n.*) trolley
tukîa (*n.*) cotton
tûku (*n.*) barrel
tûku (*v.*) pour
tûku tî esânzi (*n.*) gas tank
tûngbi (*v.*) exchange
tûngbi (*v.*) replace
tûngbi (*v.*) substitute
tunge (*v.*) support
tunngbingo (*n.*) transfer
tunngbingo-sêndo (*n.*) revolution
tunnge (*n.*) support
tunnge-ngêrë (*n.*) promotion (sale)
turûgu (*n.*) soldier

turunêe (*v.*) reverse
tutûu (*adj.*) blue
tyâa (*v.*) catch
tyâa (*v.*) trap
tyen (*n.*) tooth

ûse ... (nî) (*adj.*) second (ordinal number)
ûse ûse (*adj.phr.*) by pair (two by two)
usyo (*n.*) four

va (*n.*) servant
vakadangêre (*n.*) department store
vakando (*n.*) region
vakasinêe (*v.*) vaccinate
vakkasinengo (*n.*) vaccination
vêen (*n.*) wine
velöo (*n.*) bicycle
vêre (*n.*) glass
videö (*n.*) video
VIH (vê-î-hâsi) (*n.*) HIV
vînga-wâ (*n.*) curfew
vîsi (*n.*) screw
vizäa (*n.*) visa
vizäa tî linngo (*n.phr.*) entry visa
vo (*v.*) buy
vo (*v.*) purchase
vôte (*n.*) election
votêe (*v.*) vote
vukö (*adj.*) dark
vukö (*adj.*) black
vûko li (*v.phr.*) dye hair
vuru (*v.*) whiten
vuru (*v.*) clean (be ...)

vurü (*adj.*) white

wa (*n.*) main person concerned
wa (*n.*) owner
wâ (*n.*) fire
wâ (*n.*) heat
wâ (*adj.*) hot
wä (*v.*) advise
wä (zo) na (*v.phr.*) recommend
wâ kêtê (*adj.phr.*) warm
wâ tî irä (*n.phr.*) fire alarm
wabiandö (*n.*) fortuneteller
wabosso (*n.*) associate
wabuzze (*n.*) operator
wadakua (*n.*) officer
wadalembë (*n.*) diplomat
wadyabêti (*n.*) diabetic
wafaango-ngbanga (*n.*) judge
wafaanngo-kwayângâ (*n.*) barber
wafaanngo-papa (*n.*) referee
wafannngo-mbetti (*n.*) professor
wafanngo-mbetti (*n.*) teacher
wafanngo-pekôtenne (*n.*) interpreter
wafanngo-yê (*n.*) teacher
wafêrrere (*n.*) referee
Wafrîka (*n.*) African (n.)
wâfûe (*n.*) fireworks
wagaggango (*n.*) immigrant
wagbegibê (*n.*) suspect
wagbyanhngbingo-sû (*n.*) translator
wagerê (*n.*) pedestrian
waginnngo-nyama (*n.*) hunter
waginnngo-susu (*n.*) fisherman

wakânga (*n.*) prisoner
wakanngo-ngûme (*n.*) dairy
wakanngo-nyama (*n.*) butcher
wakanngo-yê (*n.*) seller
wakanngo-yê (*n.*) merchant
wakoba (*n.*) patient
wakoddoro (*n.*) citizen
wakoddoro (*n.*) native
Wakokö (*n.*) attorney
wakônde (*n.*) accountant
wakpalle (*n.*) guilty person
wakpê (*n.*) refugee
wakua (*n.*) worker
wakua (*n.*) agent
wakualî (*n.*) actor
wakyon (*n.*) selfish person
wala (*conj.*) or
walembë (*n.*) ambassador
waleswa (*n.*) rebel
wâlï (*n.*) female
wâlï (*n.*) woman
wâlï tî (zo) (*n.phr.*) wife
wâlï tî zo (*n.*) married woman
wâlïkua (*n.*) maid
wâlïndeko (*n.*) girlfriend
waluemäa (*n.*) tenant
wamannda (*n.*) student
wamanndango-mbetti (*n.*) student
wambanngo (*n.*) conductor
wambanngo (*n.*) guide
Wamerîka (*n.*) American (*n.*)
wamokondô (*n.*) holy
wamozoko (*n.*) musician

wamunngo-fotöo (*n.*) photograph
wandê (*n.*) foreign
wandê (*n.*) stranger
wandêlïda (*n.*) intruder
wando (*n.*) occupant
wandölikua (*n.*) staff
Wandongoro (*n.*) neighbor
wandya (*n.*) lawyer
wanganga (*n.*) doctor
wanganga (*n.*) physician
wanngo (*n.*) advice
wanzï (*n.*) thief
wanzöbê (*n.*) volunteer
Wapotto (*n.*) European
wara (*v.*) find
wara (*v.*) get
wara (*v.*) receive
wara (*v.*) welcome
wara sannzo (*v.phr.*) get infected
warrango-gene (*n.*) hospitality
wasango (*n.*) announcer
wasango (*n.*) journalist
wasarawîsi (*n.*) server
Wasarravengo (*n.*) server
wasêndâgbonngo-li (*n.*) psychologist
wasêndâ-kodëkua (*n.*) engineer
wasimbä (*n.*) traveller
wasimbä (*n.*) passenger
wasimbäfono (*n.*) tourist
wasimmba (*n.*) tourist
wasû (*n.*) author
wato (*n.*) enemy
watokua (*n.*) messenger

watonndo (*n.*) reporter
watönngo-kôbe (*n.*) cook
watumba (*n.*) terrorist
wayindä (*n.*) leader
wayinnda (*n.*) leader
wayorrongo-mabôko (*n.*) beggar
wazibba (*n.*) blind
welle (*n.*) game
wên (*n.*) arm
wên (*n.*) iron
wên (*n.*) metal
wenngo (*n.*) end
wese (*v.*) check
wese (*v.*) watch
wese-kôngbâ (*n.*) baggage check
weselinda (*n.*) check in
wesenga (*v.*) check
wesenga (*v.*) examine
wesenga (*v.*) inspect
wesesîgî (*n.*) check out
wesse (*n.*) check
wessengo (*n.*) check
wîgbê (*n.*) axle
wïkênde (*n.*) weekend
wîwên (*n.*) wire
woggbya (*n.*) queen
wokkongo (*adj.*) mild
wokkongo (*adj.*) soft
wokoso (*v.*) exploit
wokoso (*v.*) evacuate
wötarä (*n.*) grandmother
wôtoro (*n.*) bee
woza (*v.*) cancel

wu (*v.*) breathe
wu gbä (*v.phr.*) choke
wu terê (*v.phr.*) rest
wunngo (*n.*) breathing
wunngo (*n.*) number
wunngo (*n.*) quantity
wûrruru (*n.*) noise
wûrruwuru (*n.*) noise
wurukonza (*n.*) homeless

yâ (*n.*) belly
yâ (*n.*) stomach
yâ (tî zo) akânga (*v.phr.*) constipated (be ...)
Ya (zo) (*n.*) Mrs. (title)
yâda (*n.*) room
yâda komblëe (*n.phr.*) suite
yâdalinngo (*n.*) hall
yagbya (*n.*) queen (the kung's wife)
yakerre ngbonga (*n.phr.*) second (time)
yakka (*n.*) farm
yakka (*n.*) field
yakka tî lêkekke (*n.*) orchard
yäkôrâ (*n.*) pea
yamba (*adj.*) free
yamba (*adv.*) separatly
yamba (*v.*) welcome
yammbango-zo (*n.*) courtesy
yângâ (*n.*) border
yângâ (*n.*) cover
yângâ (*n.*) idiom
yângâ (*n.*) language
yângâ (*n.*) mouth
yângâ (*n.*) tip

yângâ tî Anglëe (*n.phr.*) English language
yângâ tî ngû (*n.phr.*) shore
yângâda (*n.*) door
yângâkoddoro tî wandê (*n.phr.*) foreign languages
yângâtawâ (*n.*) lid
yângbangbo (*n.*) percent
yânngangu (*n.*) coast
yassa (*n.*) fountain
yaûru (*n.*) yogurt
yê (*v.*) like
yê (*v.*) love
yê (*n.*) thing
yê (*v.*) want
yê (...) ahön (*v.phr.*) prefer
yê ake (zo) (*v.phr.*) allergy
yê kwê (*n.phr.*) anything
yê ôko äpe (*n.phr.*) nothing at all
yê terê (*v.phr.*) love each other
yê tî gô (*n.*) necklace
yê tî kua (*n.phr.*) tool
yê tî mayëre (*n.*) trick
yê tî wanî (*n.*) private property
yê tî wanî (*n.*) property
yêda (*v.*) accept
yêda (*v.*) agree
yêda (*v.*) allow
yêda na (*v.*) permit
yêda na nzöbê (*v.*) volunteer (be ...)
yêda na nzöbê (*v.phr.*) kindly accept
yeeke (*adv.*) slow
yêfûe tî gira (*n.phr.*) traditional art
yeggema (*n.*) surprise
yeke (*v.*) be

yeke na (*v.*) own
yeke ndê (*v.phr.*) be different
yeke-yeke (*adv.*) slow
yenga (*n.*) week
yenga tî dunngo (*n.phr.*) anniversary
yêngi (*v.*) move
yêngi (*v.*) rock
yenngo-daä (*n.*) acceptance
yenngo-terê (*n.*) mutual love
yêpendâ (*n.*) product
yerre (*n.*) poverty
yêwaâwa (*n.*) hazard
yindä (*n.*) direction
yinnda (*n.*) direction
yommbo (*n.*) deodorant
yommbo (*n.*) perfume
yongôro (*adj.*) long
yongôro (na nduzzu) (*adj.*) tall
yongôro kâ (*adv.phr.*) far away
yongôro kotta da (*n.phr.*) building
yôo (*v.*) carry
yôo ... ague na nî (*v.phr.*) transport (*v.*)
yoonngo(-yê) (*n.*) transportation
yoonngo-kûngbâ (*n.*) transportation of goods
yoonngo-zo (*n.*) people transportation
yoonngo-zo puse (*n.*) public transportation
yôro (*v.*) fry
yorö (*n.*) medicine
yorö (*n.*) remedy
yorö tî gasa ngo (*n.phr.*) contraceptive
yorö tî lanngo (*n.phr.*) sleeping pills
yü (*v.*) dress
yü (*v.*) wear

yurrungo (*adj.*) fluid
yuru (*v.*) flow

zamêe (*adv.*) never
zanngo wâ (*n.phr.*) flash
zanngo wâ (*n.phr.*) flashlight
zanngo wâ (*n.phr.*) light
zanngo wâ (*n.phr.*) lighting
zanngo-wâ (*n.*) ignition
zâra (*v.*) untie
zaradäa (*n.*) garden (*n.*)
zê (*v.*) warn
zêndo (*n.*) promise
zene (*v.*) skate
zenne (*n.*) skate
zenngo-ndo (*n.*) warning
zeröo (*num.*) zero
zî (*v.*) withdraw
zî yângâ (*v.phr.*) open
zîa (*v.*) allow
zîa daä (*v.phr.*) add
zîa kiri daä (*v.phr.*) tax (*v.*)
zîa na gbogbo (*v.phr.*) bedding
Zîa na luemäa (*v.phr.*) rent
zîa yamba (*v.phr.*) exclude
zîa yamba (*v.phr.*) except
zîdro (*n.*) lemon
zîngîli (*adj.*) complicated (be ...)
zingîri (*n.*) chain
zîngo (*v.*) awake
zîngo (*v.*) wake
zinngo (*n.*) withdrawal
zîpi (*n.*) zipper

zîpu (*n.*) skirt
zo (*n.*) person
zö (*v.*) burn
zö bê (*v.*) irritate
zo kîrîkiri (*n.*) anybody
zo kwê (*n.phr.*) everybody
zo kwê (*n.*) anyone
zo tî kânga (*n.phr.*) prisoner
zo tî kobêla (*n.phr.*) patient
zo tî kua (*n.*) emplpyee
zo tî kua (*n.phr.*) employee
zo tî nzï (*n.phr.*) robber
zo wa (*n.phr.*) who
zonga (*v.*) insult
zonga (*n.*) insult (*n.*)
zonga (*n.*) offense (*n.*)
zonga (*v.*) offend
zonngo (*adj.*) roasted
Zonngo (*n.*) summer
zonngo lâ (*n.phr.*) sunburn
zonyöon (*n.*) onion
zôo (*n.*) zoo
zuka (*n.*) area
zuka (*n.*) district
zuka (*n.*) area
zukayakka (*n.*) parcel
zûku to (*v.phr.*) surrender
zuty (*n.*) tool
zwâ (*n.*) island
Zwîfu (*n.*) Jew

ENGLISH-SANGO
PHRASEBOOK

Hello.
Balaô! Bara! Bara mo! (to greet one person),
Bara âla! (to greet several people)

Goodbye.
The person leaving says:

Mbï gue awe! Ngbâ nzönî! (to one person)
Âla ngbâ nzönû! (to several people)

The person remaining answers:

Gue nzönî! (to one going person)
Âla gue nzönî! (to several going people).

Yes. Iin
No. Ên-en

Do you speak English?
Mo tene Anglëe?

Excuse me.	**Excuse me.**
(to get attention)	**(to pass)**
Mbï tene?! / Appe?	Gerê tî âla kwê!

Okay.
Nzönî!

Please.
Gerê tî âla kwê / Mbï gbû gerê tî âla.
(Formal. Can be used in a colloquial setting to really
mean "I truly beg you")

BASIC PHRASES
ÂSSENGE PANDE

Thank you.
Singîla

You're welcome.
A'ke sêngê!

Sorry.
Mbï gbû gerê tî *mo* / *âla* (to one person / several people)
/ Paradôo!

It doesn't matter.
Asâra yê äpe.

I need ...
Mbï bezôa…. / Mbï yê…

Help!
Edêe mbï!

Where is the bathroom?
Ndo tî sukkukango-ngû ayeke na ndo wa?

Where is the toilet?
Dûsi ayeke na ndo wa?

Who? Zo wa?
What? Nye?
Where? Na ndo wa?
When? Lâwa
Why? Ngbanga tî nye?

entrance
linngo / lï ge
(entrance / enter here)

exit
siggingo/sïgî

open(v.) / (is open) zî / azî
closed akânga

good nzönî
bad syonî

this sô / sô ge sô	**here** ge
that sô / sô kâ sô	**there** kâ

Good morning / afternoon / evening / night.
Balaô / bara.

Good night. (when going to bed)
Lanngo nzönî.

Welcome!
Gä nzönî! / Nzönî ganngo!

How are you?
Mo yeke sêngê? / Mo 'ke sêngê?
(Talking to one person)
Âla ayeke sêngê? / Âla a'ke sêngê
(Talking to several people)

I'm fine, thank you. Iin, mbï yeke sêngê. Singîla:
And you? Ka mo? (you singular) / Ka âla? (you plural)

ÂSSENGE PANDE

• The verb *yeke* "to be" is often elided, in which case it is written with an apostrophe before the "k". In this phrasebook you will always see the options *yeke/'ke* and *ayeke/a'ke*.

See you ...
Fadë ë bâa terê ...

> **soon** ânde ma
> **later** na pekô ma
> **tomorrow** kêkerêke ma

Take care!
Dutï nzönî! / Ngbâ nzönî! (you singular) /
Âla dutï nzönî / Âla ngbâ nzönî! (you plural)

Do you speak English?
Mo tene Anglëe?

Does anyone here speak English?
Mbênî zo ge atene Anglëe?

> **I don't speak Sango.** Mbï tene Sanngo pëpe.
> **I speak only a little Sango.** Mbï tene Sanngo gï kêtê.
> **I speak only English.** Mbï tene gï Anglëe.

Do you understand? Mo mä?

> **I understand.** Mbï mä.
> **I don't understand.** Mbï mä äpe.

Could you please ...? Gerê tî mo kwê, mo lîngbi tî...?

> **repeat that** kîri mo tene tenne nî
> **speak more slowly** tene tenne nî yeeke-yeeke
> **speak louder** tene tenne nî kêtê na nduzzu
> **point out the word for me** dï mbupa nî na mbï
> **write that down** sû nî na mbï na mbetti
> **wait while I look it up** kü kêtê mbï bâa nî ge sï

What does ... mean? Ndâ tî ... ayeke nye?

How do you say ... in Sanngo?
Tî tene ... na Sanngo, a tene nye?

Arrival, Departure, and Customs
Sinngo nî, Gwenngo nî, na Passengo-duâni

I'm here . . . Mbï yeke ge…

    on vacation tî wo terê / na konzëe
    for business tî dë buzze
    to visit relatives tî bâa âsewwa
    to study tî manda mbetti

I'm just passing through.
Mbï yeke hön gï honhngo

I'm going to . . .
Mbï yeke gue na…

I'm staying at . . .
Mbï yeke lanngo na…

I'm staying for X . . .
Mbï yeke ngbâ … X.

    days lanngo
    weeks yenga / dimâsi
    months nze

- **You Might Hear**

Âla yeke na mbênî yê tî fa?
Do you have anything to declare?

Mo-wanî laâ mo kângba gbâ sô?
Did you pack this on your own?

Zî yângâ tî bozö sô. Please open this bag.

Fôko mo fûta kiri na ndö tî sô.
You must pay duty on this.

Mo yeke ngbâ tângo ôke? How long are you staying?

Mo yeke lanngo na ndo wa? Where are you staying?

I have nothing to declare. Mbï yeke na yê ôko tî fa pëpe.
I'd like to declare... Mbï yê tî fa ...

Do I have to declare this? Sô ngâ kwê, mbï du tî fa nî ?

That is mine. Sô tî mbï
That is not mine. Sô tî mbï pëpe.

This is for personal use. Sô tî mbï-wanî laâ.
This is a gift. Sô kadöo laâ.

I'm with a group. Mbï yeke na gbâ tî âzo.
I'm on my own. Mbï yeke mbï ôko.

Here is my boarding pass.
Mbetti-kamângö tî mbï laâ sô.
Here is my ID. Mbetti-fandâ tî mbï laâ sô.
Here is my passport. Passapôro tî mbï laâ sô.
Here is my ticket. Mbetti-lêgë tî mbï laâ sô.
Here is my visa. Vizäa tî mbï laâ sô.

Ticketing
Dakanngo mbetti-lêgë

Where can I buy a ... ticket?
Mbî vo *tikëe* / *mbetti-lêgë* tî... na ndo wa?

   bus bîsi/ kâra
   plane laparra
   train trëen / kpûgada

   one-way tî gwenngo nî
   round-trip tî gue tî kîri

   first class tî kubû tî âkotta-zo / tî kôzo kubû
   economy class tî kubû tî kêtê ngêrë
   business class tî kubû tî buzze

A ticket to ... please.
Mbï yê tikëe ôko tî gue na...

One ticket, please.
(Gerê tî âla kwê) tikëe ôko.

In English, people use "please" much more often than in Sango. If you want to be polite, start with *Gerê tî âla kwê*. If the situation isn't so formal, you may just ask for your ticket by saying *tikêe ôko*. If this feels rude, you can make it softer by adding *mbï yê* "I want." As a result, four choices are possible, from less polite to very polite:

Tikëe ôko. One ticket

Mbï yê tikëe ôko. I want one ticket

Gerê tî âla kwê, tikëe ôko. Please, one ticket.

Gerê tî âla kwê, mbïyê tikëe ôko.
Please, I want one ticket.

Two tickets, please.
(Gerê tî âla kwê) (mbï yê) tikëe ûse.

How much? A kä nî ôko? / Ôke?

Is there a discount for ...?
A kîri ngêrë nî na gbenî na .... äpe?

    children âmôlengê
    senior citizens âmbäkôro
    students âwamanndango-mbetti / âwamannda
    tourists âwasimmba

I have an e-ticket.
Mbï yeke na tikëe-dadä.

Can I buy a ticket on the ...?
Mbï lîngbi tî vo tikëe na yâ tî... nî?

bus bîsi / kâra
train trëen / kpûgada
boat masûa

Do I need to stamp the ticket?
Âla yê tî pîka tapöon na ndö tî tikëe nî sï?

I'd like to ... my reservation.
Mbï yê tî ... battango-mbatta tî mbï.

change gbîan   **cancel** woza   **confirm** kunisa

How long is this ticket valid for?
Tikëe nî sô angbâ nzönî tângo ôke?

I'd like to leave ...   **I'd like to arrive ...**
Mbï yê tî lonndo...   Mbï yê tî sï...

today lâsô
tomorrow kêkerêke
next week na dimâsi tî pekô
in the morning xna *ndäpêrê* / *ndën*
in the afternoon na *pekô tî bêkombïte* / *ndöh*
in the evening na lâkûi
late at night na bï

Traveling by Plane
Simmbango na laparra

When is the next flight to ...?
Mbênî laparra tî gue na... ayeke lâwa?

Is there a bus or train to the airport?
Mbênî bîsi wala trëen tî gue na gbaggba tî laparra nî
ayeke daä?

How much is a taxi to the airport?
Gwenngo na gbaggba tî laparra nî na takasy ayeke ôke?

Airport, please.
Na gbaggba tî laparra o!?
(*a rising intonation o!? expresses politeness)

My airline is ...
Mbï yeke mû... (* I'll take...)

My flight leaves at ...
Laparra tî mbï ayeke lonndo na ngbonga...

My flight number is ...
Nommoro tî hurru tî mbï ayeke...

What terminal? / What gate?
Nyötûngu wa? / Yângâda wa?

Where is the check-in desk?
Biröo tî wese linngo nî ayeke na ndo wa?

SIMBÄ NA YOONNGO-ZO

My name is ...	**I'm going to ...**
Ïrri tî mbï…	Mbï yeke gue na…

Is there a connecting flight?
Tângbi-hurru ayeke daä?

I'd like a direct flight. Mbï yê torôrô hurru.
I'd like a connecting flight. Mbï yê mbênî tângbi-hurru.
I'd like an overnight flight.
Mbï yê hurru tî bï tî sï na ndäpêrê.

How long is the layover?
Poppohuru nî ayeke nînga ngbonga ôke?

I have ...
Mbï yeke na…

> **one suitcase** sandûku ôko
> **two suitcases** sandûku ûse
> **one carry-on item** kêtê kôngbâ ôko na mabôko
> **two carry-on items** kêtê kôngbâ ûse na mabôko

Do I have to check this bag?
A yeke wese bozö sô ngâ?

How much luggage is allowed?
Kôngbâ ôke laâ zo ôko alîngbi tî gue na nî?

I'd like a window seat.
Mbï yê tî dutï na mbâgë tî finêtere

I'd like an aisle seat.
Mbï yê tî dutï na mbâgë tî batambûla

I'd like an exit row seat.
Mbï yê tî dutï na molongö tî bakpê

Can you seat us together?
Âla lîngbi tî zîa ë dutï na terê tî mbâ?

Is the flight ...?
Lapärra nî…

>   **on time** ayeke sï na tângo?
>   **delayed** adâka tângo? / amû retäar?
>   **cancelled** âla woza nî awe?

- - - - - - - - - - - - - - - - - -

You Might Hear

Zo tî pekô! Next!

Passapôro na mbetti-kamângö.
Your passport and boarding pass, please.

Tùku yâ tî bozö tî mo na gîgî. Empty your pockets.

Zî porro tî mo. Take off your shoes.

Zîa âyê tî wên kwê na yâ tî kpânngbala sembë nî.
Place all metal items in the tray.

Nommoro tî hurru … Flight number...

Nommoro tî hurru tî menngo kamângö nî fafadësô…
Now boarding flight number ...

Nommoro tî yângâda… Gate number ...

- - - - - - - - - - - - - - - - - -

Where is the baggage claim?
Âkkongba nî asïgî na ndo wa? / Kôngbâ-siggi ayeke na ndo wa?

I've lost my luggage. Kôngbâ tî mbï agirisa.
My luggage has been stolen. A nzï kôngbâ tî mbï.
My suitcase is damaged. Sandûku tî mbï abuba.

Traveling by Train
Simmbango na *trëen* / *kpûgada*

Which line goes to...Station?
Kâmbalêgë wa laâ ague na Balutti …?

Is it direct? Ague torôrô?
Is it a local train? Ayeke kpûgada tî ndurü lêgë?
Is it an express train? Ayeke kpûgada tî lorro?

I'd like to take the high-speed train.
Mbï yê tî mû kpûgada tî kotta lorro.

Do I have to change trains?
Mbï du tî tûngbi kpûgada?

Can I have a schedule?
Mbï lîngbi tî wara mbetti tî kâpälêgë?

When is the last train back?
Ndângbâ kpûgada nî ayeke kîri *lâwa*? / *na ngbonga ôke*?

Which track? *Lêgë* / *Banôn* tî sô wa?
Where is track ...? *Lêgë* / *Banôn* … ayeke na ndo wa?

Where is the dining car?
Gada tî tenngo-kôbe ayeke na ndo wa?

Where is the information desk?
Biröo tî âsango ayeke na ndo wa?

Where are the luggage lockers?
Kubû-kofforo tî âkkongba ayeke na ndo wa?

Where is the reservations desk?
Biröo tî piabattango-ndo ayeke na ndo wa?

Where is the ticket machine?
Masïni tî mbetti-lêgë ayeke na ndo wa?

Where is the ticket office?
Biröo tî mbetti-lêgë ayeke na ndo wa?

Where is the waiting room?
Bakü / Kubû tî kunngo daä ayeke na ndo wa?

This is my seat.
Sô ngendë tî mbï laâ.

Here is my ticket.
Mbetti-lêgë tî mbï lo-sô.

Can I change seats?
Mbï lîngbi tî tûngbi ngendë sêngê?

What station is this?
Sô balutti wa laâ?

What is the next station?
Balutti tî pekô ayeke sô wa?

Does this train stop at ...?
Kpûgada sô alutti na…?

TRAVEL & TRANSPORTATION
SIMBÄ NA YOONNGO-ZO

Traveling by Bus
Simmbango na *bîsi* / *kâra*

* * * * * * * * * * * * * * * * * *

> The word *bîsi* is mostly used for city buses whereas *kâra* refers most often to inter-city buses.

* * * * * * * * * * * * * * * * * *

Where is the nearest bus stop?
Balutti tî kâra/bîsi ndurü ge ayeke na ndo wa?

Which gate? Yângâda wa?   **Which station?** Balutti wa?
Which line? Lêgë wa?   **Which stop?** Arëe wa?

Can I have a bus map?
Mbï lîngbi tî wara mbênî limolêgë tî *bîsi*/*kâra*?

How far is it?
Ayo töngana nye?

How do I get to ...?
Mböi lîngbi tî sï na... töngana nye?

Which bus do I take for ...?
Kâra/*Bîsi* wa laâ mbï yeke mû tî gue na...?

Is this the bus to ...?
Bîsi/*Kâra* sô laâ ayeke gue na...?

When is the first bus to ...?
Kôzo *bîsi / kâra* tî gue na... ayeke *lâwa?* (which day)
Kôzo *bîsi / kâra* tî gue na... ayeke *na ngbonga ôke?*
(what time)

When is the next bus to ...?
Bîsi / Kâra tî pekô sô ayeke gue na ... ayeke *lâwa/na ngbonga ôke?*

When is the last bus to ...?
Ndângbâ *bîsi / kâra* tî gue na... ayeke *lâwa / na ngbonga ôke?*

Do I have to change *buses/trains?*
Mbï du tî tûngbi *kâra / kpûgada?*

Where do I transfer?
Mbï yeke tûngbi lêgë na ndo wa?

Can you tell me when to get off?
Mo lîngbi tî tene na mbï na ngbonga wa laâ ë yeke hön?

How many stops to...?
Ayeke lutti fânî ôke sï asï na...?

Where are we?
Ë yeke na ndo wa ?

Next stop, please!	**Stop here, please!**
Arëe tî pekô o!	Arëe!

Taking a Taxi
Munngo-takasy

Taxi! Takasy!

Where can I get a taxi? Mbî wara takasy na ndo wa?

Can you call a taxi? Âla lîngbi tî îri takasy?

I'd like a taxi now. Mbï yê tî wara takasy fafadësô

I'd like a taxi in an hour.

Mbï yê tî wara takasy na yâ tî ngbonga ôko.

Pick me up at ...	**Take me to...**
Mû mbï na…	Gue na mbï na…

    this address lindo sô

    the airport gbaggba tî laparra

    the train station balutti tî *kpûgada/trëen*

    the bus station balutti tî *bîsi/kâra*

Can you take a different route?

Mo lîngbi tî mû mbênî lêgë ndê?

Can you drive faster?	**Can you drive slower?**
Do wâ sï ma!	Kpë yeeke sï ma!

Stop / Wait here. Arëe. / Kü ge.

How much will it cost?	**You said it would cost ...**
A yeke fûta ânde nî ôke?	Mo tene a yeke fûta nî
	pâta…

Keep the change. Bata lamonëe nî.

Traveling by Car / Renting a Car
Simmbango na kutukutu / Luwwengo kutukutu

Where is the car rental?
A yeke luwêe kutukutu na ndo wa?

I'd like ...
Mbï yê…

a cheap car kutukutu tî kêtê ngêrë
a compact car ndurü kutukutu
a van yongôro kutukutu / kêtê kamïon
an SUV mbênî SUV
an automatic transmission
kutukutu sô ayeke gbîan lorro lo-ôko
a manual transmission
kutukutu sô ayeke gbîan lorro na mabôko
a scooter *kêtê kpûrû / sukutëre*
a motorcycle kpûrû
air conditioning *huru-dê / klimatîki*
a child seat mbatta tî môlengê

How much does it cost ...?
Ngêrë nî ôke …?

per day tî lanngo ôko
per week tî dimâsi ôko
per kilometer tî killomêtere ôko
for unlimited mileage tî sân maka
with full insurance na ngbasa-ndaû kwêzu

What kind of fuel does it use?
A yeke mû marä tî kâddawa sô wa?

SIMBÄ NA YOONNGO-ZO

Are there any discounts?
Alîngbi tî diminîi ngêrë nî?

I have an international driver's license.
Mbï yeke na peremy tî koddoro-kwêzu.

I don't have an international driver's license.
Mbï yeke na peremy tî koddoro-kwêzu pëpe.

I don't need it until ...
Mbï bezôa nî pëpe asï na …

> **Monday** Bïkua-ôko
> **Tuesday** Bïkua-ûse
> **Wednesday** Bïkua-otâ
> **Thursday** Bïkua-usyo
> **Friday** Bïkua-okü
> **Saturday** Lâpôso
> **Sunday** Lâyenga

You Might Hear

Mbï yê tî zîa nginza tî bata. I'll need a deposit.
Sù âkôzo lêsû tî irri tî mo ge. Inital here.
Kekere ge. / Sù mabôko tî mo ge. Sign here.

Fuel and Repairs
Kâddawa na Lekkengo-kutukutu

Where's the gas station?
Ndo tî kanngo-kâddawa ayeke na ndo wa?

Fill it up.
Tûku daä asï

I need...
Mbï yê…

gas kâddawa
leaded kâddawa na tungu daä
unleaded kâddawa sân tungu
regular sêngê kâddawa
super kâddawa tî süpêre
diesel Mbï yê gazwale

Check the ...
Bâa… nî

battery batery
brakes frëen
headlights âwâ tî li
oil mafùta
radiator *vunga-wâ / ladiatëre*
tail lights âwâ tî pekô
tires âpiny
transmission tunngbingo-lorro

The car broke down. Kutukutu nî akûi

The car won't start. Kutukutu nî ayeke lonndo pëpe

I ran out of gas. Kâddawa ahûnzi awe.

I have a flat tire. Gerê tî kutukutu nî akôro.

I need a ...
Mbï bezôa…

> **jumper cable** kâmba tî batery
> **mechanic** walekkengo-kutukutu
> **tow truck** kutugbongô

Can you fix the car?
Mo lîngbi tî leke kutukutu nî?

When will it be ready?
Lekkengo-nî ayeke hûnzi *lâwa?* / *na ngbonga ôke?*

Driving Around
Kpenngo na kutukutu

Can I park here?
Mbï lîngbi tî garêe ge?

Where's the parking lot?
Ndo tî garrengo-kutukutu ayeke na ndo wa?

Where's the garage? Garâzi ayeke na ndo wa?

How much does it cost?
A fûta nî ôke?

Is parking free?
A yeke fûta garrengo nî pëpe? / A garêe nzoô?

What's the speed limit?
Makalorro nî ayeke ôke?

How much is the toll?
A yeke fûta lêgë nî ôke?

Can I turn here?
Mbï lîngbi tî nguru ge?

Problems while Driving
Kpalle na gbottongo-kutukutu

There's been an accident.
Mbênî ndaû asï.

Call the police.
Îri polîsi.

Call an ambulance.
Îri ambilâsi.

My car has been stolen.
A nzï kutukutu tî mbï.

My license plate number is ...
Matrikîli tî kutukutu tî mbï ayeke...

Can I have your insurance information?
Fa na mbï mbetti tî ngbasa-ndaû tî mo?

Getting Directions
Hunndango-lêgë

Excuse me, please!
Mbï gbû gerê tî âla!

Can you help me?
Âla lîngbi tî mû na mbï mabôko?

Is this the way to ...?
Sô lêgë tî gue na … laâ?

How far is it to ...?
Tî gue na …ayo?

Is this the right road to ...?
Sô nzönî lêgë tî gue na … laâ?

How much longer until we get to ...?
Lêgë tî sï na… angbâ tî yo?

Where's ... Street? Balabâla … ayeke na ndo wa?
Where is this address? Lindo sô ayeke na ndo wa?

Where is ...
... ayeke na ndo wa?

   the highway kotta lêgë
   the downtown area vaka tî bêgalâ

Where am I?
Mbï yeke na ndo wa laâ?

Can you show me on the map?
Mo lîngbi tî fa ndo nî na mbü na lê tî limondo sô?

Do you have a road map?
Mo yeke na mbênî limolêgë?

How do I get to ...?
Mbî gue töngana nye tî sï na …?

How long does it take ...?
A yeke nînga tângo ôke…?

> **on foot** na gerê
> **by car** na kutukutu
> **by train/bus** na {*kpûgada*/*trëen*} / {*kâra* / *bîsi*}

There are two words for "train", the French loanword *trëen* and the Sango word *kpûgada*, and there are two words for "bus" both French loanwords *bîsi* and *kâra*. So you are free to use any of the following combinations for "by train / bus":

na *trëen*/*bîsi*; na *trëen* / *kâra* ; na *kpûgada* / *bîsi*; na *kpûgada* / *kâra*

I'm lost.
Mbï girisa awe.

- **You May Hear**

Gue torôrô / drowäa na dawäa. Go straight ahead.

Ngoro na kotti. Turn right.

Ngoro na gatï / gale. Turn left.

fâa balabâla across the street

ngoro gï ndo sô around the corner

na dawäa / na huzzu forward

na gbelê (tî) in front (of)

kîri na pekô backward

na pekô (tî) behind

na sangbilêgë tî pekô at the next intersection

na bengbä wâlêgë tî pekô at the next traffic light

ndurü na next to

kôzonî / kôzo tî … before

na pekô nî / na pakô tî after

ndurü ge near

yongôro kâ far

banga north

mbongo south

tö east

do west

Fâa gbagbara / pôon. Take the bridge.

Sîgî. Take the exit.

Mû kotta lêgë. Take the highway

Mû balabâla / lêgë . Take the Street / Avenue.

Mû kerebende sangbilêgë / keresangbi.
Take the traffic circle.

Where is the nearest ...?
Mbî wara mbênî … ndurü ge na ndo wa?

Can you recommend a / an ...?
Mo lîngbi tî wä mbênî …na mbï?

  hotel dagene / otêle
  inn dagene tî lêgë
  guesthouse dagene
  (youth) hostel dagene tî âmasëka

I'm looking for ... accommodations.
Mbï yeke gi ndo tî lanngo …

  inexpensive tî kêtê ngêrë
  luxurious tî pendere nî / tî kotta nginza
  traditional tî gira nî
  clean sô avuru nzönî
  conveniently located na mbênî nzönî ndo

Is there English-speaking staff?
A yeke tene Anglëe daä?

Booking a Room and Checking In
Battango-kubû na Wessengo-linngo

I have a reservation under ...
Mbï bata kubû na irri tî...

Do you have any rooms available?
Mbênî kubû angbâ sêngê na âla?

I'd like a room for tonight.
Mbï yê mbênî kubû ndâli tî bï sô.

I don't have a reservation.
Mbï bata ndo äpe.

Can I make a reservation?
Mbï lîngbi tî bata ndo?

I'd like to reserve a room ...
Mbï yê tî bata mbênî kubû...

   for XX nights tëtî bï XX
   for one person tëtî zo ôko
   for two people tëtî âzo ûse
   with a queen-size bed na kotta gbogbo tî yagbya
   with two beds na gbogbo ûse daä

How much is it? Ngêrë nî ôke?	**How much is it per night / person?** A fûta ôke tî *bi*/*zo* ôko?

Is breakfast included?
A dîko shâye kwê daä?

Does that include sales tax (VAT)?
A dîko kiri kwê daä?

Can I pay by credit card?
Mbï lîngbi tî fîta na kârâte tî kredy?

My credit card number is ...
Nommoro tî kârâte tî kredy tî mbï ayeke...

Do you have (a / an) ...?
Âla yeke na...?

air conditioning vunga-dê / klimatîki
business center bêndo tî buzze
cots lîpiköo / tangê
crib gbogbo tî bebëe
elevator ngöme / asansëre
gym dangunu
hot water ngû tî wâ
kitchen dakûku
laundry service sarawîsi tî sukkulango-bongö
linens *bongö tî ggbogbo* / daräa
microwave mikorônde
non-smoking rooms kubû sân mânga
phones sînga
pool basangû / pïsîni
private bathroom dangû tî wanî
restaurant datenngo-yê
room service sarawîsi yâ kubû
safe kofforo
television talâtu
towels suimëen
wireless Internet Gbândatere sân kâmba

Is there a curfew?
Mîngo-wâ ayeke daâ?

When is check-in?
Zo alîngbi tî linda na ngbonga ôke?

ACCOMMODATIONS

DAGENE

May I see the room?
Mbï lîngbi tî bâa kubû nî?

How can somebody call my room?
Zo alîngbi tî îri mbï na yâ tî kubû nî töngana nye?

Do you have anything ...?
Mo yeke na mbênî yê sô …?

   bigger akono ahön sô
   cleaner avuru ahön sô
   quieter ayeke sîrriri ahön sô
   less expensive ayeke kêtê ngêrë ahön sô

I'll take it.
Mbï yeke mû nî.

Is the room ready?
A leke kubû nî awe?

When will the room be ready?
Fadë a hûnzi tî leke kubû nî na ngbonga ôke?

At the Hotel

Na dagene

room number
nommoro tî kubû

floor
etâtzi (from 2ⁿᵈ floor up)
mbattana (ground floor)

room key
dafungûla / kelëe / kêrrere
tî kubû / fungûla-kubû

Where is the ...?
... ayeke na ndo wa?

> **bar** bâar
> **bathroom** dangû / dûsi
> **convenience store** magazäni ndurü ge
> **dining room** datenngo-yê
> **drugstore/pharmacy** dayorö / dakanngo-yorö
> **information desk** *mêzä tî sango* / *ndosango*
> **lobby** kubûlinngo / dalinngo
> **pool** ngûlando / pisîni
> **restaurant** dakôbe / datenngo-yê
> **shower** dûsi / dangû / da tî sukkulango-ngû

Can I have (a) ...?
Mbï lîngbi tî wara mbênî...?

> **another room key** ûse dafungûla
> **blanket** balangëti
> **clean sheets** vurrungo dräa
> **pillow** koli
> **plug for the bath** kpodadä tî sukkulango-ngû
> **soap** savöon / kpön
> **toilet paper** kugbë tî kabiny
> **towels** suimëen

I would like to place these items in the safe.
Mbï yê tî zîa âyê sô na yâ tî kofforo.

I would like to retrieve my items from the safe.
Mbï yê tî zî âyê tî mbï na yâ tî kofforo.

DAGENE

Can I stay an extra night?
Mbï lîngbi tî ngbâ lanngo ôko na ndönî?

Problems at the Hotel
Kpalle na Dagene

There's a problem with the room.
Mbênî kpalle ayeke na kubû nî.

The ... doesn't work.
… atambûla pëpe.

> **air conditioning** *vunga-dê / klimatîki* nî
> **door lock** dafungûla tî kubû nû
> **hot water** ngû tî wâ nî
> **shower** dûsi nî
> **sink** pepengû nî
> **toilet** kabiny nî

The lights won't turn on.
Âwâ nî azä pëpe.

The ... aren't clean.
… ayeke saratëe.

> **pillows** âkoli nî
> **sheets** âdaräa nî
> **towels** âsuimëen nî

The room has bugs / mice.
Ânnanderre/Âdeku ayele na yâ tî kubû nî.

The room is too noisy.
A yeke mä wûrruwuru na yâ tî kubû nî mîngi.

I've lost my key.
Kêrrere tî mbï agirisa

I've locked myself out.
Mbï kânga yângâda nî na kêrrere nî na yâ nî.

Checking Out
Wese tî sîgî

When is check-out?
A yeke wese tî sîgî na tângo wa?

When is the earliest I can check out?
Kôzo ngbonga sô mbï lîngbi tî wese tî sîgî daä ayeke
sô wa?

When is the latest I can check out?
Ndângbâ ngbonga sô mbï lîngbi tî wese tî sîgî daä
ayeke sô wa?

I would like to check out.
Mbï yê tî wese tî sîgî.

I would like a receipt.
Mbï yê tî wara risy.

I would like an itemized bill.
Mbï yê tî wara mbetti-fûta na nzîna nî.

DAGENE

There's a mistake on this bill.
Mbeti-fûta sô ayeke na lêgë nî pëpe.

Please take this off the bill.
Mbï gbû gerê tî âla, âla zî sô na yâ tî mbeti-fûta nî.

The total is incorrect.
Kotta wunngo nî ayeke na lêgë nî pêpe.

I would like to pay ...
Mbï yê tî fûta ...

   by credit card na kârâte tî kredy
   by (traveler's) check na syêki (tî wasimbä)
   in cash na dedêe nginza

Can I leave my bags here until ...?
Mbï lîngbi tî zîa âbozö tî mbï ge asï na...? .

Renting Accommodations
Luwwengo-da

I'd like to rent (a / an) ...
Mbï yê tî luwêe...

   apartment yâdayamba
   house da
   room kubû

How much is it per week?
A fûta nî ôke na dimâsi ôko ôko?

I intend to stay for XX months.
Mbï yê tî ngbâ daä nze XX.

Is it furnished?
A luwêe na kôongbâ kwê daä?

Does it have (a / an) ...?   Does it include (a / an) ...?
Ayeke na ... kwê daä?   A luwêe nî na ... kwê daä?

   cooking utensils âggbakuru tî tonngo-yê
   dishes âsembê
   dryer gbara-bongö
   kitchen dakûku
   linens âdaräa
   towels suimëen
   washing machine masïni tî sukkulango-bongö

Do you require a deposit?
Fôko mbï zîa nginza sï?

When is the rent due?
A yeke fûta luwemäa nî na lanngo wa?

Who is the superintendent?
Kotta wandombe nî ayeke zo wa?

Who should I contact for repairs?
Zo wa laâ ayeke bâa lêgë tî lekkengo âyê sô abuba?

Camping and the Outdoors
Kinngo-barra ngâ na Duttingo na gîgî polêlê

campsite lêndobarra

Can I camp here?
Mbï lîngbi tî ki barra ge?

Where should I park?
Mbï lîngbi tî garêe kutukutu na ndo wa?

Do you have ... for rent?
Mo yeke na.... tî luwemäa?

cooking equipment gbâkkuru tî tonngo-yê
sleeping bags bozollanngo
tents dabongö

Do you have ...
... ayeke daä?

electricity Wâ tî *dadä / kuräan*
laundry facilities Lêgë tî sukûla bongö
showers *Ndo tî sukûla ngû / Dûsi*

How much is it per ...?
Ngêrë tî ... öko ayeke ôke ?

lot gbâ nî   person zo   night bï

Are there ... that I should be careful of?
Âmmbeni yê ayeke daä töngana..., sô mbï du tî sâra
hânge na nî?

animals	insects	plants
ânyama	ânnzekede	âkonngo yê

Meals
Marä tî kôbe

breakfast shâye / kôbe tî ndäpêrê
lunch (kôbe tî) midy
dinner kôbe tî lâkûi
snack *kôbe tî ndölitï* / *hânda-nzara*
dessert desëre

Types of Restaurants
Âmarä tî datenngo-kôbe

bar bâar	**kosher restaurant**
bistro danyonngo	datenngo-kôbe tî kasyere
buffet *saravêe-terê* / *bifëe*	**pizzeria** dapizza
café dakâwa	**restaurant** datenngo-kôbe /
fast food restaurant	dakôbe /datê
kôbe-hîo / sotëe	**snack bar** bâar datê
halal restaurant	**teahouse** dasâi
datenngo-kôbe tî halâla	**vegetarian restaurant**
	dakôbe sân nyama

Can you recommend ...?
Mo lîngbi tî wä na mbï mbênî…?

   a good restaurant nzönî *datenngo-yê* / *datê*
   a restaurant with local dishes
   datenngo kôbe tî koddoro
   an inexpensive restaurant datenngo-yê tî kêtê ngêrë
   a popular bar nganda sô âzo ague daä mîngi

Reservations and Getting a Table
Piabattango-ndo na warrango mêzä

I have a reservation for ...	The reservation is under ...
Mbï bata ndo ge ndâli tî…	Battango-ndo nî ayeke na irri tî…

I'd like to reserve a table for ...
Mbï yê tî bata mêzä ndâli tî…

Can we sit ...?
Ë lîngbi tî dutï …?

> **over here** na mbâgë ge
> **over there** na mbâgë kâ
> **by a window** ndurü na finêtre
> **outside** na gîgî
> **in a non-smoking area**
> na mbênî ndo *sô a nyön mânga daä pëpe* / *sân mânga*

How long is the wait?
Ë yeke kü anînga?

Ordering
Kommandengo-kôbe

It's for here. / It's to go.
Ayeke tî te ge. / Ayeke tî gue na nî.

Waiter/Waitress!	Excuse me!
Saravëre!	Mbï gbû gerê tî âla!

I'd like to order.
Mbï yê tî komandêe.

Can I have a ... please?
Âla gä na mbï... o!?

  menu motarâka tî âkôbe nî
  wine list motarâka tî âsämba nî
  drink menu motarâka tî nyonngo-yê
  children's menu motarâka tî kôbe tî âmôlengê

Do you have a menu in English?
Âla yeke na mbênî motarâka na Anglëe?

Do you have a set / fixed price menu?
Kanza tî kôbe / Kôbe sô ngêrë tî gbânî gï ôko ayeke daä?

What are the specials?
Kotta pendere kôbe tî âla aayeke nye?

Do you have ...?
Âla yeke na...?

Can you recommend some local dishes?
Mo lîngbi tî wä na mbï mbênî nzönî kôbe tî koddoro?

What do you recommend?
Sô wa laâ mo wä nî na mbï?

I'll have ...
Fadë mbï mû...

Can I have a ...?
Mbï lîngbi tî wara…?

    glass of ... vêre tî…
    bottle of ... ngbennda tî…
    pitcher of ... nduttu tî…

What's this?
Sô nye laâ?

What's in this?
Nye laâ na yâ tî sô?

Is it ...?
Ndôngô ayeke daä? (*Is hot pepper in it?)

    spicy aso
    sweet anzere
    bitter asêe
    hot ayeke wâ
    cold adë

Do you have any vegetarian dishes?
Kâsa tî kugbë sân nyama ayeke daä?

I'd like it with ...
Mbï yê nî na…

I'd like it without ...
Mbï yê nî sân…

red wine bengbä vêen
white wine vurü vêen
rosé wine rozëe
palm wine kangoya / pekë
dessert wine vêen tî desëre
dry wine kurru vêen

A light beer, please.
Gä na mbï yappungo
byêre o!?

A dark beer, please.
Gä na mbï vukö byêre o!?

Special Dietary Needs
Âkûne tenngo-yê

I'm on a special diet.
Tenngo-yê tî mbï ayeke ndê

Is this dish free of animal product?
A tö kâsa sô na mbênî yê tî terê tî nyama daä äpe?

I'm allergic to ...
... ayê mbï äpe.

I can't eat ...
Mbï lîngbi tî te... pëpe.

dairy kôbe tî ngû tî me
eggs parra
gelatin mafüta tî koso / zelatîni
gluten glutêni
meat nyama
nuts kurru lê tî kekke
peanuts kârâkö
seafood nyama tî *lamêre* / *ngûnyamma*
spicy foods kôbe tî ndôngô
wheat farïni

I'm diabetic.
Mbï yeke na dyabêti.

Do you have any sugar-free products?
Âla yeke na mbênû kôbe sân sukâni?

Do you have any artificial sweeteners?
Âla yeke na mbênî nzerekâsa kpa-yorö?

I'm vegan/vegetarian.
Mbï yeke watenngo *gï kugbë tî kâsa* / *kâsa sân nyama.*

Complaints at a Restaurant
Demmango na datenngo-yê

This isn't what I ordered.
Sô laâ mbï komandêe äpe.

I ordered ...   This is ...
Mbï komandêe...   Sô ...

cold adë
undercooked amü nzönî äpe
overcooked amü ahön ndönî
spoiled abuba awe
not fresh anîkkpiri awe / anzêen awe
too spicy aso na ndôngô mîngi
too tough akpêngba mîngi
not vegetarian ayeke kugbë tî kâsa pëpe

Can you take it back, please?
Kîri na nî o!?

I cannot eat this.
Mbï lîngbi tî te sô äpe.

How much longer until we get our food?
Kôbe nî ayeke gä ânde lâwa?

We cannot wait any longer.
Ë lîngbi tî kü mbênî pëpe.

We're leaving.
Ë yeke hön tî ë.

Paying at a Restaurant
Futtango-yê na datenngo-yê

Check, please!
Gä na mbï mbetti-fûta nî.

We'd like to pay separately. Ë yê tî fûta ndê ndê.
Can we have separate checks?
Ë lîngbi tî wara mbetti-fûta ndê ndê?
We're paying together. Ë yeke fîta kwê ôko.

Is service included?
A dîko sarawîsi nî daä?

What is this charge for?
Fûta tî sô nî sô ayeke ndâli tî nye?

There is a mistake in this bill.
A yûu ndo na yâ tî mbetti-fûta sô

I didn't order that. I ordered ...
Mbï komandêe sô pëpe. Mbï komandêe…

Can I have a receipt, please?
Mbï lîngbi tî wara risy nî?

Can I have an itemized bill, please?
Mbï lîngbi tî wara mbetti-fûta na nzîna nî?

It was delicious!
Kôbe nî alogoma!

Cooking Methods
Ângôbo tî tonngo-kôbe

baked zö na fûru	**re-heated** tö pekô nî
boiled kporo na ngû	**roasted** zö töngana suîya
braised zö na lê tî wâ	**sautéed** yôro na sotëe
breaded zö na fuku	**smoked** tö na gurru
creamed tö na kâddangûme	**steamed** tö na mböwâ
diced fâa na zegë	**stewed** tö na ngû
filleted fâa asîgî kâmba	**stir-fried** yôro na sotëe
grilled zö na nzânge	**stuffed** mboma
microwaved tö na mïkrônde	**toasted** yôro
poached tö na bozö nî	

rare hânda-wâ
medium rare tö na hânda-wâ amü ndâmbo nî
well-done tö amü nzönî

on the side zö na terê-wâ

Tastes
Nzereyângâ

bitter sesêe	**sour** kpikpîi
bland yugbe	**spicy** na nzerekâsa
salty na hîngö	**sweet** logo-logo

Dietary Terms
Âmbupa tî kûne tenngo-yê

decaffeinated sân kaffeîni
free-range sô a bata na gîgî
genetically modified sô a gbîan ngoangoa nî
gluten-free sân glutêni
kosher kasyere
low-fat na kêtê mafûta
low in cholesterol na kêtê mafûta-mênë
low in sugar na kêtê *sûkere / ngâakô*
organic tî saterê
salt-free sân hîngo
vegan watenngo-gï-kugbë
vegetarian watenngo-kâsakugbë

Breakfast Foods
Kôbe tî shayêe

coffee kâwa
bread mâpa
butter dubêre / matenge
milk ngûme
porridge potopôto
eggs parra
honey lavu
jam / jelly kpatta / kpatta-logo
omelet yorrongo parra
yogurt yaûru

Vegetables
Ålenngo kâsa / Åkugbëkâsa

amaranth gbudu
avocado avokäa
bean gbolë / arikôo
bean leaf kûlî
cabbage shûu
cassava leaf ngunzä
cassava tuber kpanngaba
carrot kärôte
coleus (Gnetum Africanum) koko
coreta (Corchorus olitorius (Tiliaceae) gûsâ / gôsâ
corn nzö
cucumber kukkuru
cucurbita kôsö
garlic lâi
green amaranth (Amaranthus viridis) gbudu
ground peas gbôkkora
lentils kêtê hariköo
lettuce saläde
mushrooms guggu
okra vekë
onion zoyöon
peas lê / lêlê
pepper ndôngô
potato pommbotêre
pumpkin kawoya
radish rady
solanium aethiopicum ngâgö

spinach epinäar
sweet potato bäbolo
tomato tomâte
yam gwî

Fruits and Nuts
Lê tî kekke na lê tî kâsa

amomum
(Aframomum africanum) (Zingliberaceae) kôpya / tonndo
apple pômo
banana fondo
cashew kêrêwere
coconut koköo / lê tî koköo
cola gôro
date tâmuru
grapefruit pommbolomûsu
guava goyâvo
lemon bengbä zîdoro
lime zîdoro
mandarin mandarîni
mango mângo
orange ndîmon / zorânde
papaya papâi
peanut kârâkö
pineapple ananäa / zananäa
plum lêngunngu
safut safû
sesame sindi
starfruit pakapâka

sugar cane ngâakô
tangerine mandarîni
watermelon kawoyangû / passatêke

Meats
Âkâsa tî nyama

> Add *nyama tî* "meat of" to specify that you are
> talking about the meat of the animal.

beef (nyama tî) bâgara
chicken kôndo
duck kanäna / libêbe
goat ngäsa
lamb nyîtäba
pork (nyama tî) koso / gaduru
rabbit ndaramba
steak yorrongo nyama
veal (nyama tî) nyîbâgara / môlengê tî bâgara

Seafood
Âkâsa tî lamêre

(There is no sea in the CAR, so the following names
refer to animals that live in river water).

crab kângbâ
fish susu
shrimp dikkinzi

Desserts
Desëre

cake gatöo
ice cream galâsi
pastries makala

pie kpatta
porridge potopôto

DRINKS
Nyonngo-yê

Non-alcoholic drinks
Nyonngo-yê sân sämba

coffee (black) kâwa / sêngê kâwa
coffee with milk kâwa na ngûme
hot chocolate shokoläa tî wâ nî
lemonade ngûzîdoro / limmonâde
milk ngûme / dulëe
mineral water ngûtênë
orange juice ngûndîmon / ngû tî zorânde
sparkling water ngûsodäa
soda / soft drink sodäa
soymilk ngû tî sozya
tea sâi / dutëe

Alcoholic drinks
Âsamba

beer byêre
   bottled beer byêre tî ngbennda
   canned beer byêre tî kopo
   draft beer byêre tî pombëe
brandy ngbâko / ârêge
champagne champagne / syampânye
cocktail kokkotêle
gin dyîni
liqueur ngangü sämba
margarita maragarîta
martini maratiny
rum rômo / lômo
scotch wisiky
tequila tekiläa
vermouth veremûtu
vodka vodokäa
whisky wisiky
wine vêen / divëen
   dessert wine vêen tî desëre
   dry wine kurru vêen
   red wine bengbä vêen
   rosé wine rozëe
   white wine vurü vêen

Grocery Shopping
Vonngo-nzerekâsa na magazäni

Where is the nearest market / supermarket?
Dakannngo-yê / magazäni ayeke na ndo wa ndurü ge?

Where are the baskets / carts?
Âsakpä / Âkady ayeke na ndo wa ?

I'd like some of this / that.
Mbï yê *sô / sô kâ.*

Can I have ...?
Mbï yê…

> **a (half) kilo of ...** (ndâmbo) kilöo ôko tî…
> **a liter of ...** lîtiri ôko tî…
>
> **a piece of ...** mbênî *fângbi / li* tî… ôko
> **two pieces of ...** mbênî *fângbi / li* tî… ûse
>
> **a little more / less** mbênî kêtê na *ndöni / gbeni.*

Can I have a little of ... please?
Mbï lîngbi tî wara mbênî kêtê *yângâ/mbâgë* tî….?

Can I have a lot of ... please?
Mbï lîngbi tî wara … nî gbânî?

That's enough, thanks.
Alîngbi awe! Singîla.

TENNGO-YÊ NA NYONNGO-YÊ

Where can I find ...?
Mbï lîngbi tî wara ... na ndo wa?

    cleaning products ângûsavöon tî sukkulango-ndo
    dairy products âkôbe tî ngûme
    delice section mbâgë tî kanngo tonngo-kâsa
    fresh produce finî kâsa
    fresh fish finî susu
    frozen foods kpenngba dedêe kâsa
    household goods âggbakuru tî gbû na yâda
    meats ânyama / âsade / âsa
    poultry ândeke / âkôndo

I need to go to the ...
Fôko mbï gue na...

    bakery dakanngo-mâpa
    butcher shop dakanngo-nyama
    convenience store magazäni tî *terêda* / *ndongoro*
    fish market *galâ tî susu* / *galâsusu*
    produce market galâ tî âkôbe tî yakka
    supermarket kotta magazäni

Paying for Groceries
Futtango-galâ

Where is the checkout?
Ayeke fûta na ndo wa tî sïgî?

Do I pay here?
Mbï fûta ge?

Do you accept credit cards?
Mbï lîngbi tî fûta na kârâte tî kredy?

I'll pay in cash.
Mbï yeke fûta na dedêe nginza.

I'll pay by credit card.
Mbï yeke fûta na kârâte tî kredy.

Paper/Plastic, please.
Mû na mbï *kugbë/nilöon*, o?

I don't need a bag.
Mbï bezôa bozö äpe.

I have my own bag.
Mbï yeke na bozö tî mbï awe.

Where can I exchange money?
Mbï lîngbi tî sanzêe nginza na ndo wa?

Is there a currency exchange office nearby?
Mbênî ndo tî sannzengo nginza ayeke ndurü ndosô?

I'd like to exchange ... for ...
Mbï yê tî sanzêe… na …

US dollars doläar tî Amerîka
pounds *pôndo*/*nginza* tî Anglëe
Canadian dollars doläar tî Kanadäa
Euros Eröo
traveler's checks syêki tî wasimbä
CFA franc farânga CFA
coin of 5 CFA francs pâta

What is the exchange rate?
Mbäli tî sannzengo nî ayeke ôke?

What is the commission charge?
A fûta ôke tî sannzengo-nî ?

Can you write that down for me?
Sû nî kwê na mbetti na mbï, o?

Banking
Labânge

Is there a bank near here?
Mbênî labânge ayeke ndurü ge?

Where is the nearest ATM?
Mbênî masïni tî gbottongo-nginza ayeke ndurü ge?

What time does the bank open / close?
Labânge nî ayeke *zî/kânga* na ngbonga ôke?

Can I cash this check here?
Âla lîngbi tî fûta na mbï syêki sô ge?

I would like to get a cash advance.
Mbï yê tî wara mbâgë tî nginza nî ne dedêe nî kôzonî sï.

I would like to cash some traveler's checks.
Mbï yê tî kä âmmbeni âsyêki tî mbï tî wasimbä tî wara na dedêe nginza.

I've lost my traveler's checks.
Syêki tî mbï tî wasimbä agirisa.

The ATM ate my card.
Masïni tî gbottongo-nginza nî amene kârâte tî mbï.

Shopping
Vonngo-yê

Where's the ...?
... ayeke na ndo wa?

    antiques store dakanngo ângbêre yê
    bakery dakanngo-mâpa
    bookstore dakanngo-bûku
    camera store dakanngo-fotöo / dakanngo-kameräa
    clothing store dakanngo-bongö
    convenience store dakanngo-yê ndurü gë
    delicatessen dakanngo-loggoma
    department store kotta magazäni
    electronics store dakanngo âmasïni-dadä
    gift shop dakanngo-kadöo
    health food store dakanngo âkôbe tî sênî
    jeweler dakanngo-lenge na âyê tî pendere
    liquor store dakanngo ângangü sämba
    mall kêtê-galâ
    market galâ
    music store dakanngo-mozoko / damozoko
    pastry shop dakanngo-gatöo
    pharmacy dakanngo-yorö / dayorö
    shoe store dakanngo-porro / daporro
    souvenir store dakanngo âyê tî däbê
    supermarket kotta magazäni
    toy store dakanngo âyê tî ngyâ

Getting Help at a Store
Hunndango-mabôko na yâ tî dakanngo-yê

Where's the ...?
... ayeke na ndo wa?

cashier kêsi
escalator ngarangâra
elevator ngömezûu
fitting room *käbîni* / *kubû* tî tarrango-bongö
store map limondo tî magazäni

Can you help me?
Mû na mbï mabôko o!? / Edêe mbï o!?

I'm looking for ...   Where can I find ...?
Mbï yeke gi…   Mbî wara… na ndo wa?

I would like ...
Mbï yê…

I'm just looking.
Mbï yeke bâa gï ndo baanngo.

Preferences
Yê sô apîka bê tî zo

I want something ...
Mbï yê mbênî…

- **big** kotta yê
- **small** kêtê yê
- **cheap** yê tî kêtê ngêrë
- **expensive** yê tî kotta ngêrë
- **local** yê tî koddoro nî ge
- **nice** *yê tî pendere* / *pendere yê*

I can only pay ...
Mbï lîngbi tî fûta gï…

Is it authentic?
Ayeke taâ pîri nî?

Can you show me that? | Can I see it?
Fa sô mbï bâa? | Fa nî mbï bâa.?

Do you have any others?
Mo yeke na âmbênî töngasô?

Can you ship this? | Can you wrap this?
Mo lîngbi tî tokua sô? | Mo lîngbi tî kânga sô?

Do you have this in ...?
Mo yeke na sô na… nî?

black vukö	**orange** bengbä kambîri
blue tutûu	**pink** rôzi
brown ngbôn	**purple** dammbili
gray mburuwâ	**red** bengbä
green ngunzä /	**white** vurü
ngûngunzä	**yellow** kambîri

Do you have anything lighter?
Mo yeke na mbênî sô avuru kêtê ahön sô?

Do you have anything darker?
Mo yeke na mbênî sô avûko kêtê ahön sô?

Haggling at a Store
Pikkango pattara tî ngêrë na yâ tî dakanngo-yê

That's too expensive.
Ngêrë nî aso mîngi.

Do you have anything cheaper?
Mo yeke na mbênî yê tî kêtê ngêrë äpe e!?

I'll give you ...
Mbï yeke mû na mo…

I'll have to think about it.
Mbï gbû li tî mbï daä sï.

Is that your best price?
Kôtê nzönî ngêrë tî mo nî kwê laâ?

Can you give me a discount?
Kîri nî na gbenî kêtê na mbï ma!

Deciding
Kunningo-bê

That's not quite what I want.
Tî bê tî mbï laâ kwê kwê äpe.

I don't like it.
Mbï yê nî äpe.

It's too expensive.
Ngêrë nî aso mîngi.

I'll take it.
Mbï yeke mû nî.

Paying at a Store
Futtango-yê na yâ tî magazäni

Where can I pay?
A yeke fûta na ndo wa?

How much?
Ôke?

Does the price include tax?
A dîko ndoggo nî sô na
kiri kwê daä?

I'll pay in cash.
Mbï yeke fûta na dedêe nginza.

I'll pay by credit card.
Mbï yeke fûta na kârâte tî kredy

Do you accept traveler's checks?
Âla yeke mû syêki tî wasimbä?

I have a / an ...
Mbï yeke na …

   ATM card kârâte tî labânge
   credit card kârâte tî kredy
   debit card kârâte tî *fâa-nginza* / *kudda*
   gift card kârâte tî kadöo

Can I have a receipt?
Mbï lîngbi tî wara risy?

Complaining at a Store
Demmango na yâ tî magazäni

This is broken.   **It doesn't work.**
Sô afâa awe.   Atambûla äpe.

I'd like ...
Mbï yê …

   to exchange this tî *sanzêe* / *tùngbi* sô
   to return this tî kîri na sô
   a refund a kîri nginza nî
   to speak to the manager tî bâa *kotta-ndombe* /
   manazëre nî

Services
Âsarawîsi

barber wafaanngo-kwayângâ
dry cleaner wamboonngo-bongö
hair salon dafaanngo-li / dafaanngo kwa tî li
laundromat damasïni tî sukkulango-bongö
nail salon danzenne / da tî lekkengo-nzenne
spa dawâmbö / sapäa
travel agency dasimbä

At the Hair Salon / Barber
Na *dafaanngo-li / dafaanngo-kwayângâ*

I'd like a ...
Mbï yê…

   color a vûko li tî mbï
   cut a fâa li tî mbï
   perm li-sêkü
   shave a kîon li tî mbï
   trim a fâa ndöbê tî li tî mbï

Cut about this much off.
Fâa gbâ tî sô kwê.

Can I have a shampoo?
Mbï lîngbi tî wara shampween?

Cut it shorter here.   Leave it longer here.
Fâa sô ge ndurü.   Zîa sô ge ayo.

At a Spa
Na *sapäa/dawâmbö*

I'd like a / an ...
Mbï yê…

> facial mboonngo-lê
> manicure kyonngo-mabôko
> massage nikkango-terê
> pedicure kyonngo-gerê
> wax menngbo
> aromatherapy ngangayommbo
> acupuncture ngangaswa
> sauna sonäa / dangûwâ

At a Laundromat
Na terê tî masïni tî sukkulango-bongö

Is there full-service?
Âla laâ ayeke saravêe zo?

Is there self-service ?
Zo ôko ôko laâ ayeke saravêe terê tî lo?

Is there same-day service?
A hûnzi kua nî na lâ ôko?

Do you have ...?
Âla yeke na…

> bleach zyavêle
> change lamonëe
> detergent zîbibbila

> dryer sheets
> kugbë tî hollengo-yê
> fabric softener
> yorö tî wôko na bongö

This machine is broken.
Masïni sô akûi awe.

How does this work?
Sô atambûla töngana nye?

When will my clothes be ready?
Bongö tî mbï nî ayeke hûnzi lâwa?

whites âvurï bongö
colors âbongö tî nzorôko
delicates âzezêe bongö

hand wash âbongö tî sukûla na mabôko
gentle cycle gini yeeke
permanent press pete sêkü / pasêe kpengü
dry clean only a sukûla gï na mbö / a mbôo mboonngo

cold water dedêe ngû / ngû tî dê
warm water ngû sô amû wâ kêtê / tyêtyê ngû
hot water ngû tî wâ

Hello. Bala ô!
Hi! Bara ma!
Welcome! Gä nzönî!
Good morning / afternoon / evening. Bala ô!
Good night. Lanngo nzönî.

Sir Pakara / Mesie
Madam Yapakara / Madäma
Mr. Pkr.
Ms. Msk.
Mrs. Yazo / Ya
Dr. (medical) Nganga / Dokotöro / Dok.
Dr. (academic) Dokotöro / Dok.

What's your name? **My name is ... And you?**
Irri tî mo zo wa? Irri tî mbï…. Ka mo?

How are you?
Töngana nye?

Fine, thanks. **And you?**
Yê a'ke äpe! Ka mo?

See you ...
Fadë ë bâa terê… ma!

   later na pekô
   soon ânde
   tomorrow kêkerêke

TENNENGO-TENNE NA ZO

Goodbye.
Gue nzönî (to the person who is going away) /
Ngbâ nzönî (to the person who remains back)

Please.
Gerê tî mo kwê! (talking to one person)
Gerê tî âla kwê! (talking to several people)

Thank you.	**You're welcome.**
Singîla!	Ayeke sêngê!

I'm sorry.
Mbï gbû gerê tî *mo* / *âla*
(talking to one person / to several people).

Excuse me.
Paradôo a'ke.

Where are you from?   I'm from ...
Mo yeke zo tî koddoro wa? Mbï yeke zo tî…

Algeria Alazery
Angola Angoläa
Benin Benëen
Burkina Faso Burkina Faso
Burundi Burundi
Cameroon Kamerûne
Chad Tyâde
Central African Republic Bêafrîka / Koddorosêse tî
Bêafrîka
Congo (The Republic of) Kongö (Koddorosêse tî)
Congo (The Democratic Republic of the) Kongö
(Koddorosêse tî Ngunuhalëzo tî K.)
Egypt Ezîpita
Erytrea Eritrëe
Ethiopia Etiopy
Eswatini Eswatini
Gabon Gaböon
Gambia Gambï
Equatorial Guinea Ginëe tî Ekuatëre
Guinea / Guinea-Conakry Ginëe / Ginëe-Konakîrî
Guinea-Bisau Ginëe-Biso
Lesotho Lesoto
Liberia Liberïa
Madagascar Madagasikära
Mali Maly
Mauritania Moritany
Mauritius Mörîsi

Morocco Marôko
Namibia Namiby
Niger Nizëre
Nigeria Nizerïa
Rwanda Ruandäa
Senegal Senegäle
Saychelles Seysyêle
Sierra Leone Sierra Leöne
Somalia Somaly
South Africa Afrîka-Mbongo / Afrîka tî Mbongo

* * * * * * * * * * * * * * * * * *

To refer to the whole southern region of Africa,
say *Mbongo ti Afrika.*

* * * * * * * * * * * * * * * * * *

Sudan Sudäan
Southern Sudan Sudäan-Mbongo / Sudäan tî
Mbongo
Tunisia Tunizy
Togo Togöo
Zambia Zamby
Zimbabwe Zimbabwe
Australia Osotraly
Canada Kanadäa
England Angletëre
Ireland Irrilânde
Iceland Issilânde
New Zealand Finî Zelânde
the United States (of America) Âkanza koddoro tî
Amerîka / Amerîka
the United Kingdom Koddorogbya-Ôko

I'm ...
Mbï yeke …

Algerian Zo tî Alazery / Waalazery
Angolan Zo tî Angoläa / Waangoläa
Beninese Zo tî Benëen / Wabenëen
Burkinabe Zo tî Burkina Faso / Burkinabë / Waburkina
Burundese Zo tî Burundi / Waburundi
Cameroonian Zo tî Kamerûne / Wakamerûne
Chadian Zo tî Tyâde / Watyâde
Central African Zo tî Bêafrîka / Wabêafrîka
Congolese Zo tî Kongö / Wakongö / Kongö
Egyptian Zo tî Ezîpita / Waezîpita / Wazîpita
Erytrean Zo tî Eritrëe / Waeritrëe / Waritrëe
Ethiopia Zo tî Etiopy / Waetiopy / Watiopy
Eswatinian Zo tî Eswatini / Waeswatini / Waswatini
Gabonese Zo tî Gaböon / Wagaböon
Gambian Zo tî Gambï / Wagambï
Equatorial Guinean Zo tî Ginëe tî Ekuatëre / Waginëe tî Ekuatëre
Guinean / Conakry-Guinean Zo tî Ginëe (tî Konakîrî) / Waginëe (tî Konakîrî)
Bisau-Guinean Zo tî Ginëe-Biso / Waginëe-Biso
Lesotho Zo tî Lesoto / Walesoto / Soto
Liberian Zo tî Liberïa / Waliberïa
Malagasy Malagâsi
Malia Zo tî Maly / Wamaly
Mauritanian Zo tî Moritany / Wamoritany
Mauritius citizen Zo tî Mörîsi / Wamörîsi

Moroccan Zo tî Marôko / Wamarôko
Namibian Zo tî Namiby / Wanamiby
Nigerien Zo tî Nizëre / Wanizëre
Nigerian Zo tî Nizerïa / Wanizerïa
Rwandese Zo tî Ruandäa / Waruandäa
Senegalese Zo tî Senegäle / Wasanagäle
Seychellese Zo tî Seysyêle / Waseysyêle
Sierra Leonese Zo tî Sierra-Leöne / Wasierra-leöne
Somalian Zo tî Somaly / Wasomaly
South African Zo tî Afrîka-Mbongo / Zo tî Afrîka tî Mbongo / Waafrîka-mbongo / Waafrîka tî Mbongo
Sudanese Zo tî Sudäan / Wasudäan
Southern Sudanese Zo tî Sudäan tî Mbongo / Wasudäan tî Mbongo
Tunisian Zo tî Tunizy / Watunizy
Togolese Zo tî Togöo / Watogöo
Zambian Zo tî Zamby / Wazamby
Zimbabweian Zo tî Zimbabwe / Wazimbabwe
American Zo tî Amerîka / Waamerîka
Australian Zo tî Osotraly / Waosotraly / Wasotraly
Canadian Zo tî Kanadäa / Wakanadäa
English Anglëe
Irish Zo tî Irrilânde / Wairrilânde
a New Zealander Zo tî Finî Zëlânde / Wafinî-Zëlânde
Scottish Zo tî Ekôsi / Waekôsi

Where were you born?	I was born in ...
A dü mo na ndo wa?	A dü mbï na...

This is my ...
Sô... tî mbï.

husband kôlï	**older brother** yayâ
wife wâlï	**younger**
partner ndeko	**brother** ngambe
mother mamâ	**older sister** yayâ
father babâ	**younger sister** ngambe

cousin (*like brother and sister) îtä

aunt (*father's sister, and children of her brother) hömba

uncle (*mother's brother, and children of his sister) kôya

grandmother âta / âta-wâlï / tarä

grandfather âta / âta-kôlï / tarä

mother-in-law kôgarâ / mamâ (You can call your mother-in-law *mamâ* to show respect.)

father-in-law kôgarâ / babâ (You can call you're your father-in-law *babâ* to show respect.)

brother-in-law (*and sister-in-law, both younger than oneself. If they are older than oneself, they are called *kôgarâ* like father-in-law and mother-in-law) moyen

sister-in-law moyen

step-mother mamâ

step-father babâ

step-sister (*called and considered just as a genuine "sister") îtä (tî mbï) tî wâlï (*Literally: "sibling (of me) as female" = my sister / my step-sister)

step-brother îtä (tî mbï) tî kôlï (*Literally: "sibling (of me) as male" = my brother / my step-brother)

SALLANGO-NZAPÄ

What religion are you?
Mo yeke sâra nzapä tî nye?

I am agnostic.
Mbï hînga Nzapä äpe.

I am atheist.
Mbï mä bê na Nzapä äpe.

I am…
Mbï yeke…

> **Buddhist** wabudäa
> **Catholic** kattolîki
> **Christian** keretyen
> **Hindu** hindü
> **Jewish** zuîfu
> **Muslim** mizilimy

Do you like ...?
Mo yê… .?

   art yêfûe
   cinema sindimäa / sinimäa
   music mozoko
   sports ngyângunu
   theater ngbadârâ

Yes, very much.   **Not really.**
Iin, mbï yê nî mîngi.   Kwê kwê äpe.

A little.
Kêtê.

I like ...   **I don't like ...**
Mbï yê…   Mbï yê… äpe.

Can you recommend a good ...?
Mo lîngbi tî wä na mbï mbênî nzönî…

   book bûku
   CD sêdêe (CD)
   exhibit fafâ
   museum dambeso
   film filimo
   play ngyâ

What's playing tonight?
Nye laâ âla yeke *pika* / *fa* na lâkûi sô?

I like ... films / movies.
Mbï yê *âfîlimo* / *âsinimäa* tî...

> action sallango-yê ngangü
> art yêfûe
> comedy ngyâ
> drama ye tî ngangü
> foreign kaddoro wandê
> horror sa-mbeto
> indie Mangaläa / Ênnde
> musical mozoko
> mystery yê tî ndimâ
> romance bolingo
> suspense yeggema

What are the movie times?
Sinimäa nî ayeke na ngbonga ôke?

Sports
Ngyângunu

I like ...
Mbï yê ...

> basketball ndembö tî nzânge
> bicycling kpenngo na *velöo* / *gbâzâbängâ*
> boxing gobo
> diving sanngo-gbengû
> golf gôlôfo
> hiking simmbango
> martial arts ngyâtiri

soccer   ndembö tî gerê
swimming   sanngo-ngû
tennis   tënîsi
volleyball   ndembö tî gbânda

When's the game?
A yeke pîka ndembö nî lâwa?

Would you like to go to the game with me?
Mo yê ë na mo ë gue na ndembö nî?

What's the score?
A *pîka* / *zîa* ngû nî ôke?

Who's winning?
Zo wa laâ asö benda?

Do you want to play?
Mo yê tî pîka ndembö nî?

Can I join in?
Mbï lîngbi tî linda ngyâ nî?

What are your plans for ...?
Mo pialeke tî sâra nye …?

> **tonight** na bï sô
> **tomorrow** kêkerêke
> **the weekend** na *pôsöyenga* / *wikênde*

Would you like to get a drink?
Mo yê tî nyön mbênî yê?

Where would you like to go?
Mo yê tî gue na ndo wa?

Would you like to go dancing?
Mo yê tî gue tî dö dô?

I'm busy. Mbï yeke na kua.	**That sounds great!** Sô taâ nzönî.
No, thank you. Ên-en, singîla!	**Go away!** Hön kâ!
I'd like that. Iin! Mbï yê mîngi tî gue.	**Stop it!** Angbâ ndo sô!

I'm here with my ...
Mbï yeke ge na… tî mbï.

> **boyfriend** ndeko
> **girlfriend** ndeko
> **husband** kôlï
> **wife** wâlï
> **partner** ndeko
>
> **friend(s)**
> îtä (sing.) / âytä (pl.) /
> fombâ (sing.) /
> âfombâ (pl.)

A friend can be called *îtä* "brother/sister", *fombâ* "comrade", or *sonngo* "relative/kin".

I'm ...
Mbï yeke…

   single kombammba
   married na kôlï / na wâlï (with a man / with a woman)
   separated na lêgë tî kângbi
   divorced divorsëe / kângbi awe
   seeing someone bâa mbênî zo

Can I kiss you?
Mbï lîngbi tî su yângâ tî mo?

I like you.
Mbï yêkia mo.

I love you.
Mbï yê mo.

Mail
Tonngo-mbetti

Where is the post office?
Datokua ayeke na ndo wa?

Can I buy stamps?
Mbï yê tî vo têmbere?

I would like to send a ...
Mbï yê tî tokua…

> **letter** mbetti
> **package / parcel** koly
> **postcard** kugbëlimo

Please send this via ...
Mbï yê tî tokua nî na…

> **air mail** laparra
> **registered mail** rekomandëe / sûpendâ
> **priority mail** kpëkpesë
> **regular mail** sêngê tokua

It's going to ...
Ayeke gue na…
(See list of countries, pg. 253)

How much does it cost?
Ngêrë nî ayeke ôke?

When will it arrive?
Ayeke sï lâwa?

It contains ... What is ...?
... ayeke na yâ nî. ... ayeke nye?

> **your address** lindo tî mo
> **the address for the hotel** lindo tî *dagene/otêle* nî
> **the address I should have my mail sent to**
> lindo sô âzo adu tî tokua mbetti tî mbï daä

Can you write down the address for me?
Sû lindo nî na mbï na mbetti, o!?

Is there any mail for me?
Mbï wara mbênî mbetti?

international tî koddoro wandê
domestic tî *kpôkömâa / yâ tî koddoro ge*
(literally: for *locally/inside of the country here*).
postage binngo na datokua
stamp tapöon
envelope bozommbeti
postal code nommoro tî datokua
customs duâni
postal insurance ngbasa-ndaû tî datokua

Telephones
Sînga

Where is a pay phone?
Kubûsînga ayeke na ndo wa?

Can I use your phone?
Mbï lîngbi tî îri ndo na sînga tî mo?

I would like to ...
Mbï yê tî…

    make an overseas phone call
    îri ndo yongôro na koddoro wandê
    make a local call
    îri ndo ge na *koddoro nî ge* / *kpôkömâa*
    (the country here / locally)
    send a fax tokua *fàkisi* / *sîngasûkô*

What number do I dial for ...?
Mbî pîka nommoro wa tî wara…?

    information sango
    an outside line sînga tî gîgî
    an operator walenngo-sînga

What is the phone number for the ...?
Nommoro tî sînga tî…. ayeke nye?

    hotel dagene / otêle
    office ndokua / biröo
    restaurant datenngo-yê / datenngo-kôbe
    embassy dalembë

What is your ...?
… ayeke nye?

    phone number nommoro tî sînga tî mo
    home phone number nommoro tî sînga tî mo tî da
    work phone number nommoro tî sînga tî mo tî kua
    extention (number) nommoro tî ndâsînga tî mo

fax number nommoro tî *sîngasükô* / *fâkisi* tî mo
cell phone number nommoro tî sînga tî mo tî bozö

Can you write down your number for me?
Sû na mbï nommoro tî sînga tî mo na mbetti o!?

My number is ...
Nommoro tî sînga tî mbï ayeke…

What is the country code for ...?
Nommoro tî koddoro tî… ayeke nye?

I would like to buy a / an...
Mbï yê tî vo…

> **domestic phone card**
> kârâte tî pîka sînga na *koddoro nî ge* / *kpôkömâa.*
> **international phone card**
> kârâte tî pîka sînga na koddoro wandê.
> **disposable cell phone** bibîi sînga
> **SIM card** kârâte SIM
> **cell phone recharge card** kredy na yâ tî sînga tî mbï
> **pre-payed cell phone** piafûta sînga tî bozö

What is the cost per minute?
Ngêrë tî nzîna ngbonga ôko ayeke ôke?

I need a phone with XX minutes.
Mbï yê sînga na nzîna ngbonga XX daä.

How do I make calls?
Mbî pîka sînga töngana nye?

COMMUNICATIONS
TONNGBINGO-LÖ

collect call mû sînga
toll-free nzoô
phonebook bûkusînga
voicemail tokua *tî yângâ / gô*

On the phone
Na ndö tî sînga

Hello?
Alô? / Mallo!

* * * * * * * * * * * * * * * * * *

The person who calls always says *Alô?*. The
person who receives the call also says *Alô?*, but
uses *Mallo!* if the caller is important or of a
higher rank.

* * * * * * * * * * * * * * * * * *

Hello. This is ...   May I speak to ...?
Alô? ... laâ!   Mbï yê tî tene tenne na...

... isn't here; may I take a message?
... ayeke daä äpe. Ala yê tî zïa tokua na lo?

I would like to leave a message for ...
Mbï yê tî zîa tokua na...

Sorry, wrong number.
Paradôo, nommoro nî laâ äpe.

Please call back later.
Gerê tî âla kwê, âla kîri aîri ndo na pekô.

I'll call back later.
Fadë mbï kîri mbï îri ndo *ânde/na pekô*.

Bye.
Ë sâra töngasô.

Computers and the Internet
Kombûta na gbândatere

Where is the nearest ...?
Mbênî ... ayeke ndurü ge?

Internet café dakâwa tî gbândatere
computer repair shop dalekkengo-kombûta

Do you have ...?
Âla yeke na...

available computers kombûta sô angbâ sêngê
(wireless) Internet gbândatere (sân kâmba)
a printer masïni-petesû
a scanner eskanëre / forolimo

How do you ...?
A ... töngana nye?

turn on this computer zä kombûta sô
log in linda daä
connect to the wi-fi tângbi na wify
type in English pîka na Anglëe

COMMUNICATIONS
TONNGBINGO-LÖ

How much does it cost for ...?
Ngêrë tî … ayeke ôke?

> **15 minutes** nzîna ngbonga 15
> **30 minutes** nzîna ngbonga 30
> **one hour** ngbonga ôko

What is the password?
Pafubgûla nî ayeke nye?

My computer ...
Kombûta tî mbï …

> **doesn't work** atambûla äpe
> **is frozen** akukuta
> **won't turn on** alonndo pëpe
> **crashed** akûi awe
> **doesn't have an Internet connection**
> atângbi na Gbândatere pëpe

computer kombûta
laptop kpânngbala kombûta
USB port dûtângbi USB
ethernet cable kâmba Ethernet
CD sêdêe (CD)
DVD dêvvedêe (DVD)
telegram mbettisînga
e-mail sîngambetti
e-mail address sîngalindo

Professions and Specializations
Kodëkua na kûne kua

What do you do?
Mo yeke sâra kua tî nye?

I'm a/an ...
Mbï yeke ...

accountant wakônde
admisistrative assistant kotti walenngo-kua
aid worker waeddengo-zo
architect wasêndâkinngo-da
artist wakuafûe
assistant kotti-wakua
banker wabânge
businessman/businesswoman wabuzze
carpenter sarapandëe
CEO Pêddezêe (PDG)
clerk watonndo tî dangbanga
consultant wawanngo tî kodëkua
construction worker wakinngo-yê
contractor wadenngo-buzze
coordinator wadonngbingo-kua
dentist nganga-pemmbe
director wayindä / wayinnda
doctor nganga / wanganga / dokotöro
editor waseppengo-sû
publisher wadavunnga

electrician wakua tî kuräan / wakuräan / wasêndâkuräan (*For "worker in electricity" say "wakua tî kuräan / wakuräan", but for "a specialist in electricity" say "wasêndâkuräan")

engineer wasêndâ-kodëkua

intern wamanndango-kua

journalist wasango

lawyer wandya

librarian wakanngo-mbetti

manager walenngo-kua / ndombe

nurse wabattango-forôto / seyä

politician waporosö

secretary wakuasû

student wamannda / wamanndango-yê

supervisor walindökua

teacher wafanngo-yê / wafanngo-mbetti (teacher of anything / schoolteacher)

writer wasunngo-mbetti

I work in ...
Mbï yeke sâra kua (na yâ) tî ...

academia kaddami

accounting sênndakônde

advertising denngo-saggba

the arts sênndafûe

banking sênndabânge / sêndâlabânge

business sêndâbuzze

education sêndâfanngo-mbetti

engineering sêndâkodëyê

finance sêndânginza

government govvoroma / ngurugbya
journalism sêndâsango
law sêndândya
manufacturing sêndâmasïni-kua
marketing sêndâgalâ
the medical field sêndânganga
politics sêndâporosö
public relations sêndâtonngbingo-lö puse
publishing sêndâvunnga
a restaurant datenngo-yê
a store dakanngo-yê / magazäni
social services sarawîsi na terê tî âzo
tourism simbäfono
travel buzze tî simbä / simbä

Business Communication and Interaction
Tôngbilö tî denngo-buzze na pattara

I have a *meeting/ appointment* with ...
Mbï yeke na *kâpä / kunngo-kâpa* na ...

Where's the ...?
... ayeke na ndo wa?

business center kubû tî buzze
convention hall yâda tî kotta bûngbi
meeting room kubû tî bûngbi daä

Can I have your business card?
Mbï lîngbi tî wara mmbetti-buzze tî mo?

Here's my name card.
Mbetti-danditëe tî mbï laâ.

I'm here for a ...
Mbï gä ndosô ndâli tî...

    conference tôngbilö
    meeting bûngbi
    seminar bûngbi tî kua / kâpäkua

My name is ...
Irri tî mbï ...

May I introduce my colleague ...?
Zîa mbï fa fombâkua tî mbï ... na *âla*/ *mo*?
(to *you* [plural] / *you*[singular])

Pleased to meet you.
Gä nzönî / Nzönî.

I'm sorry I'm late.
Paradôo, sô mbï sï na tângo äpe sô.

You can reach me at ...
Mo lîngbi tî wara mbï na...

I'm here until ...
Mbï yeke na ndo sô asï na...

I need to ...
Mbï yê tî... / Fôko mbï...

> **make a photocopy** sâra sûkôlimo / fotokopy
> **make a telephone call** îri ndo na sînga
> **send a fax** tokua sîngasûkô / fâkisi
> **send a package (overnight)** tokua koly
> (tîtene asï kêkerêke)
> **use the Internet** sâra kua na Gbândatere

It was a pleasure meeting you.
Anzere na mbï tî wara *âla/mo*.

I look forward to meeting with you again.
Mbï yê mîngi tî kîri tî wara *âla/mo*.

- - - - - - - - - - - - - - - - - - - -

You Might Hear

Singîla sô mo gä sô. Thank you for coming.

Kü kêtê sï, o!? One moment, please.

A kü kâpä na mo? Do you have an appointment?

Zo wa? With whom?

Lo... He / She ...

> *yeke na bûngbi* is in a meeting
> *yeke na simbä tî buzze* is on a business trip
> *hön na konzëe* is away on vacation
> *sîgî fafadësô* just stepped out
> *yeke ngbâ na terê tî mo* will be right with you
> *yeke wara mo fafadësô* will see you now

Âla dutï sï ma. Please have a seat.

- - - - - - - - - - - - - - - - - - - -

Business Vocabulary
Âmbupa tî denngo-buzze

advertisment saggba
advertising denngo-saggba
bonus matabïsi
boss sêfu / patröon
briefcase bozobbuze / bozö-buzze / bozö tî buzze
business buzze
business card mbettibuze
business casual (dress) sêngê *bongobbuze* / *bongö-buzze*
business plan gbarrabuze
casual (dress) sêngê bongö
cell phone number nommoro tî sînga tî bozö
certification kunnisangyo
certified sô a kunisa nî awe / pekunisa
colleague fombâkua
company lakoppya
competition mandako
competitor wamandako
computer kombûta
conference tôngbilö
contract mbere
course sêngêrë
cubicle käbîni
CV sêvêe (CV) / pendâdûnîa
deduction dirringo-yê
degree ndoto / degrëe
desk mêzä / biröo
employee wakua / zo tî kua

employer patröon / wangassengo-zo

equal opportunity passa-litûtu

expenses futtango-yê / kanngo-nginza

experience hanngo-lê / hinngango-yê

fax number nommoro tî *sîngasùkô / fâkisi*

field yakka

formal (dress) sapëe

full-time tângo kwê / mêkê tângo

global mobimba

income nginzalinda

income tax kiri tî nginzalinda / lapôo tî nginzalinda

insurance ngbasa-ndaû

job kua / kusâra

joint venture têngbi-buzze / tenngbingo-buzze

license (mbetti) zîlêgë / lisâsi / peremy

mailing tonngo-mbetti

marketing sêndâgalâ

meeting bûngbi / warrango-terê / mïtîngi
(Say "bûngbi" for a meeting involving a crowd,
"warrango-terê" for a private meeting with a few
friends, and "mïtîngi" for an political public meeting)

minimum wage ndângbâ kêtê fûta

multinational dabuzze tî âkoddoro-kôte

office biröo / ndokua

office phone number nommoro tî sînga tî *ndokua/ biröo*

paperwork gbâ tî mbetti-kua

part-time mbâgë-tângo

printer masïni-petesû / sasango

profession kusâra / kua / kuatê

professional tî wakodëkua / tî wakuatê

project pialö
promotion yaanngo na nduzzu / pussungo
raise menngo
reimbursement kîringinza
resume fanngo-terê ndurü / ndurü tenne
salary nginza tî kua / ûta
suit kazâka
tax ID nîfi
tie karavâte
trade fair galâ tî kusâra / galâkua
uniform maräbongö
union bûngbi
visa vizäa
wages nginza tî kua / fûta
work number nommoro tî kua / nommoro tî buzze
work permit peremy tî kua

AT THE DOCTOR
Na danganga

Making an Appointment
kunngo-kâpä

Can you recommend a good doctor?
Mo lîngbi tî wä na mbï mbênî nzönî wanganga?

I'd to make an appiontment for ...
Mbï yê tî kü kâpä tenne tî…

  today lâsô
  tomorrow kêkerêke
  next week dimâsi tî pekô
  as soon as possible kôzo lêgë sô azî

Can the doctor come here?
Wanganga nî alîngbi tî gä ge?

What are the office hours?
Biröo/Ndokua nî azî na ngbonga ôke?

It's urgent!
Ayeke yê tî ngangü! / Âla gä hîo sï!

I need a doctor who speaks English.
Mbï yê mbênî wanganga sô atene anglëe.

How long is the wait?
Fadë ë kü anînga?

MEDICAL
SÊNDÂNGANGA

Ailments
Kôbe na kâsa

I have allergies.
Terê tî mbï ake âmmbeni yê.

I have an allergic reaction.
Terê tî mbï asara / asûku / alë / abe.
(Literally: My body itches / swells / makes buttons / gets red.)

I have arthritis.
Ngëbiö aso mbï.

I have asthma.
Mbï yeke na pâsi tî wunngo.

I have a backache.
Pekô tî mbï aso sonngo.

I have bug bites.
Âmanderre ate mbï.

I have chest pain.
Kate tî mbï aso sonngo.

I have a cold.
Dê asâra mbï na korro.

I have cramps.
Dadä agbû mbï.

I have diabetes.
Mbï yeke na dyabêti.

I have diarrhea.
Mbï sasa.

I have the flu.
Mbï yeke na palüh.

I have an earache.
Mê tî mbï aso sonngo.

I have a fracture.
Biö tî mbï akûngbi.

I have a fever.
Mbï yeke na *fyêvre* /
dê-yâ-ndowâ.

I have a heart condition.
Mbï yeke na kobêla tî bê.

I have high blood pressure.
Mbï yeke na tasyoon. / Mênë tî mbï akpê hûo mîngi.
(*I have blood pressure / My blood runs too fast)

I have low blood pressure.
Mênë tî mbï akpë yeeke mîngi.

I have an infection.
Mbï wara sannzo.

I have swelling.
Terê tî mbï asûku.

I have indigestion.
Mbï wara sonngo-yâ na
kôbe.

I have a sprain.
Terê tî mbï anôno.

I have a stomachache.
Yâ tî mbï aso sonngo.

I have pain.
Yê ayeke so mbï.

I have sunburn.
Lâ azö mbï.

I have a rash.
Terê tî mbï asara mbï.

MEDICAL
SÊNDÂNGANGA

I have sunstroke.
Lâ aso li tî mbï.

I have a toothache.
Pemmbe tî mbï aso sonngo.

I have a urinary tract infection.
Mbï sâra hînön na sannzo.

I have a venereal disease.
Mbï yeke na kobêla tî mîterê.

I need medication for ...
Mbï yê mbênî yorö ndâli tî…

I'm anemic.
Mênë tî mbï ayeke mîngi äpe.

I am constipated.
Yâ tî mbï akânga na kôbe.

I am dizzy.
Li tî mbï *agini / aturunêe.*

I am bleeding.
Mênë tî mbï ayeke yuru.

I am having trouble breathing.
Mbï wu nzönî äpe. / Mbï wu gbä.

My period is late.
Yâ tî mbï akânga.

I've been sick for ... days.
Terê tî mbï aso, lanngo…

I am nauseous.
Bê tî mbï alonndo.

It hurts here.
Aso ge.

I am pregnant.
Mbï yeke na ngo.

It's gotten worse.
Aso ahön tî kôzo

I am vomiting.
Mbï yeke dë.

It's gotten better.
Asavâa kêtê.

You Might Hear

Wu ngangü. Breathe deeply.

Tïko. Cough, please.

Zî bongo. Undress, please.

Aso ge? Does it hurt here?

Hä yângâ tî mo. Open your mouth.

Nzönî mo bâa mbênî kûne wanganga.
You should see a specialist.

Nzönî mo gue na danganga/lopitäni.
You must go to the hospital.

Afâa awe. / Abuba awe. It's broken.

Avunga kobêla. / Abi kobêla na terê tî zo. It's contagious.

Abibila awe. / Asâra sannzo awe. It's infected.

Anôno. It's sprained.

Kîri mo gä na dimâsi ûse. Come back in two weeks.

Fôko a bâa pekô tî mo. You need a follow-up.

Treatments and Instructions
Munngo-yorö na âmbella

Do I need a prescription medicine?
Mbï bezôa mbênî mbella tî munngo-yorö ?

Can you prescribe a generic drug?
Mo lîngbi tî sû na mbï mbella tî gegere yorö?

Is this over the counter?
A lîngbi tî vo sô yamba sêngê?

How much do I take?
Mbï mû nî ôke?

How often do I take this?
Mbï yeke mû nî fânî ôke?

Are there side effects?
Pâsi tî *pekô/terê* nî ayeke daä?

Is this safe for children?
Âmôlengê alîngbi tî mû nî sêngê?

I'm allergic to ... ... ayê mbï äpe.

antibiotics fâafi /antîbyo	**aspirin** assipirîni
anti-inflammatories	**codeine** koddeîni
mîngowâ / antîwâ	**penicillin** pennisilîni

* * * * * * * * * * * * * * * * * * * *

You Might Hear

Mbï yeke sû na mo mbella tî... I'm prescribing you ...

fâafi / antîbyo antibiotics
fâa-senneki / fâa-makongö anti-virals
hinni an ointment
dessongo painkillers

Fôko... You need ...

a bâa/ tondo yâ tî mênë tî mo a blood test
a kpo mo ba tonga an injection
a pepenga mo an IV
a bâa yâ tî mênë tî mo ndâli tî senne-lenge a strep test
a bâa/ tondo yâ tî hinö tî mo a urine test

* * * * * * * * * * * * * * * * * * * *

Payment and Insurance
Futtango-nî ngâ na ngbasa-ndaû

I have insurance.
Mbï yeke na ngbasa-ndaû.

How much does it cost?
Ngêrë nî ôke?

Do you accept ...?
Âla yeke mû…?

Can I have an itemized receipt for my insurance please?
Mbï lîngbi tî wara mbênî risy na nzîna nî ndâli tî ngbasa-ndaû tî mbï?

Can I pay by credit card?
Mbï lîngbi tî fûta na kârâte tî kredy?

Will my insurance cover this?
Ngbasa-ndaû tî mbï ayeke mû sô?

At the Optometrist
Na ndo tî wanganga-mekalê

I need an eye exam.
Mbï yê sï a tondo lê tî mbï

I've lost ...
… agirisa.

  a lens *langilê* / *langi* tî mbï ôko
  (*langilê* = eye-lens, *langi* = lens)
  my contacts âlangilê tî mbï
  my glasses tatarra tî mbï

Should I continue to wear these?
Mbï ngbâ gï tî yü sô tî gue na nî?

Can I select new frames?
Mbï lîngbi tî soro mbênî finî gbâzâ nî?

How long will it take?
Ayeke mû tângo ôke?

I'm nearsighted / farsighted.
Mbï yeke bâa ndo gï *ndurü* / *yongôro*.

At the Dentist
Na ndo tî wanganga-pemmbe

This tooth hurts.	I have a toothache.
Pemmbe sô aso sonngo.	Pemmbe tî mbï aso sonngo.

I have a cavity.
Mbï yeke na dû na yâ tî pemmbe tî mbï.

I've lost a filling.
Tungu tî pemmbe tî mbï afâa atï.

My tooth is broken.
Pemmbe tî mbï afâa.

Can you fix these dentures?
Mo lîngbi tî leke na mbï *gbâzâpemmbe* / *gbâzâtyen* sô?

My teeth are sensitive.
Pemmbe tî mbï amä sonngo mîngi.

You Might Hear

Fôko a pete tungu na yâ tî dù tî pemmbe tî mo. / Mo bezôa pettengo-tungu. You need a filling.

Mbï yeke kpo mo na tonga / faanngo-sonngo tî ndo ôko. I'm giving you an injection/a local anesthetic.

Fôko mbï gbôto pemmbe sô. I have to extract this tooth.

Kü ngbonga ... awe sï mo te mbênî yê. Don't eat anything for ... hours.

At the Gynecologist
Na ndo tî wanganga-ndâwâlï

I have cramps.
Dadä agbû mbï.

My period is late.
Mbï bâa yâ tî mbï äpe. / Mbï bâa nze äpe.

I have an infection.
Mbï wara kassanzo.

I'm on the Pill.
Mbï yeke nyön pilîli.

I'm not pregnant.
Mbï yeke na ngo äpe.

I'm ... months pregnant.
Mbü yeke na (ngo tî) nze...

My last period was ...
Ndângbâ baanngo yâ tî mbï ayeke na...

I need ...
Mbï yê tî wara…

   a contraceptive mbênî gasa-ngo
   the morning-after pill pilîli tî ndadë nî
   a pregnancy test gi-sêngo
   an STD test gi-gbanakoba

At the Pharmacy
Na dayorö/dakanngo-yoröö

Where's the nearest (24-hour) pharmacy?
Dakanngo-yorö ndurü ge (sô azî ngbonga 24) ayeke na
ndo wa?

What time does the pharmacy open / close?
Dayorö nî ayeke zî / kânga na ngbonga ôke?

Can you fill this prescription?
Mo lîngbi tî sûnzi mbettimbela nî?

How long is the wait?
Ayeke nînga tângo ôke?

I'll come back for it.
Fadë mbï kîri ndâli nî.

What do you recommend for (a / an) ...?
Nye laâ mbï lîngbi tî mû ndâli tî…?

   allergies ângassara
   cold dê na korro
   cough tîkö

diarrhea sasa
hangover pendâsämba / pendânyonngo
motion sickness *denngo na kutukutu / ngassimba*
post-nasal drip yurrungo ndâhôn
sore throat sonngo yâgô
upset stomach sonngo yâ / lonndongo bê

Do I need a prescription?
Mbï bezôa mbettimbela?

I'm looking for ...	**Do you have ...?**
Mbï yeke gi …	*Mo* / *Âla* yeke na…?
	(mo *sing.* / âla *pl.*)

(parfum of) aftershave (yommbo tî) pendâkyonngo
anti-diarrheal kâi-sasa
antiseptic rinse sukûla-pendâsorro
aspirin assipirîni
baby wipes yângâbongö tî bebëe / bongö-ngbondâ
tî bebëe
bandages bânde
cold medicine dedêe nganga
a comb suali
conditioner yorö tî *wôko* / *hasa* li
condoms sosêti / bozönâ
cotton balls ligbâ tî *tende*/*kotöon*
dental floss *wîtyen* / *wîpemmbe* / *kâmba tî pemmbe*
deodorant fâafîon / tomba-fîon
diapers kûsi
gauze gâzi / komprêsi
a hairbrush borôsi tî li

hairspray pisipîsi tî li
hand lotion hinni tî mabôko
ibuprofen ibûporrofêni
insect repellant tomba-ngungu / tomba-nzêkkede
moisturizer fimamyon
mousse (hair) lusu kwali
mouthwash sukkulango-yângâ
razor blades lâmo / lazwaar
rubbing alcohol alakôlo tî nika terê
shampoo shampween
shaving cream savöon tî kyonngo-kwa
soap savöon / kpön
tampons tapöon
a thermometer sâandowâ
throat lozenges yâpugô
tissues bongo / bânde
toilet paper kugbë tî kabiny
a toothbrush *kpaka-pemmbe / borôsi tî pemmnbe*
toothpaste *kpattapembe / kpatta tî pemmbe*
vitamins vittamîni

abdomen yâ	**gland** lêkûtu
anus nyerë	**hair** kwali
appendix lênngere	**hand** mabôko / tï
arm tï / mabôko	**heart** bê /gonda
back ndöbê / pekô	**hip** ndâkunni
belly button tûrûngu	**intestines** vi / mvi
bladder bozö-hînön	**jaw** *biö tî ngbângbâ /*
bone biö	*biö-ngbângbâ*
buttocks ngbondâ	**joint** litângbi / ngëwê
breast me	**kidney** lêlê
chest kate	**knee** likunni
ear mê	**knuckles** litângbi / ngëwê
elbow ngotti	**leg** gerê
eye lê	**lip** *porronyo / porro tî*
face lê	*yângâ*
finger litï	**liver** bê / bebe
foot gerê	**lung** fufû

mouth yângâ / (nyö/nyô)
(the common word is *yângâ* but *nyö /nyô* occurs much
more frequently in compound words)

muscle sade / sa	**stomach** vi / sêtâ
neck gô	**testicles** kolobô
nose hôn	**thigh** kunni
penis kennge / nâ	**throat** dûgô / pepegô
rectum dünyerë	**thumb** tälitï
rib *biökate / biö tî kate*	**toe** ligerê
shoulder ndotti	
skin porro	

tooth/teeth
pemmbe / âpemmbe
tyen / âtyen
tongue mennga
tonsils âmïngôrô
urethra pepehînön
uterus dabambî
vagina dondö
vein pepesisa
waist gbëyâ
wrist ligobo

Help!
Mbï kûi o! / Âzo âla gä o!
(lit. I am dying! / People, you Come, please!)

Fire!
Dagbï o! / Wâ o!

Thief!
Zo tî nzi! / Wanzi! Âla gbû lo!
(lit. Thief! / You catch him!)

Police!	**Leave me alone!**
Polîsi!	Zîa mbï (kpô)!
It's an emergency!	**There's been an attack!**
Kpëkpesë!	A dûga ndo.
Stop!	**There's been an accident!**
Awe! / Angbâ ndosô!	Ndaû asï.

Call ...!
Âla îri… hîo!

   an ambulance ambilâsi
   a doctor nganga / dokotöro
   the fire department *âdagbï* / *ndokua tî âdagbï*
   the police polîsi

Is anyone here ...?
Mbênî zo ge…?

   a doctor ayeke wanganga / dokotöro
   trained in CPR amanda kodë tî zîngo bê na fufû

GENERAL EMERGENCIES
KPËKPESË KWÊZU

Quickly!	Be careful!
Hîo sï!	Hânge!

Where is the ...?
… ayeke na ndo wa?

American embassy Dalembë tî Amerîka
bathroom *ndo tî sukûla ngû / dûsi*
hospital lopitäni / labatäni
police station ndokua tî polîsi

Can you help me?
Mû na mbï mabôko o!?

Can I use your phone?
Zîa mbï îri ndo na sînga tî mo o!?

I'm lost.	Go away!
Mbï girisa lêgë awe. /	Hön kâ!
Mbï yû ndo awe.	

Talking to Police
Tennengo-tenne na polîsi

I've been ...
Âzo …

assaulted adûga mbï
mugged apîka mbï
raped alanngo na mbï na ngangü
robbed anzï mbï
swindled anzï mbï na yâ tî buzze

That person tried to ... me.
Zo sô atara tî ...

    assault dûga mbï
    mug pîka mbï
    rape lanngo na mbï na ngangü
    rob nzï mbï

I've lost my ...	My ... was stolen.
Mbï girisa ... tî mbï	A nzï .... tî mbï

    bag(s) bozö
    credit card kârâte tî kredy
    driver's license peremy
    identification mbetti-danditëe
    keys dafungûla / kêrrere
    laptop kpângbala kombûta
    money nginza
    passport passapôro
    visa vizäa
    wallet bozöpâta / portomonëe

I've lost my ...	My ... was stolen.
Mbï girisa ...	A nzï ....

    purse bozö tî mbï tî mabôko
    traveler's checks syêki tî mbï tî wasimbä

I need a police report.
Mbï bezôa tonndo tî polîsi.

Please show me your badge.
Âla fa na mbï palâta tî âla.
(Use *âla* for you instead of *mo* to show politenesss)

Please take me to your superior / the police station.
Gue na mbï na mbênî kotta kâmba / na ndokua tî polîsi.

I have insurance.
Mbï yeke na ngbasa-ndaû

This person won't leave me alone.
Zo sô ayê tî zîa mbï kpô pëpe.

My son / daughter is missing.
Môlengê tî mbï tî *kôlï / wâlï* agirisa.

He / She is XX years old.
Lo yeke na ngû XX.

I last saw the culprit XX minutes / hours ago.
Mbï bâa wasanna nî asâra *nzîna ngbonga / ngbonga* XX.

| **What is the problem?** | **What am I accused of?** |
| Tenne nî ayeke nye? | Syonî tî nye laâ mbï sâra? |

I didn't realize that it wasn't allowed.
Andâa ndya ake sô? Mbï hînga fadë äpe!

| **I apologize.** | **I didn't do anything.** |
| Mbï gbû gerê tî âla! | Mbï sâra yê ôko äpe! |

I'm innocent.
Mbï yeke tî mbï mabôko-vurü.

I need to make a phone call.
Fôko mbï îri ndo na sînga.

I want to contact my embassy / consulate.
Mbï yê tî îri *dalembë* / *dagbelembë* tî mbï.

I want to speak to a lawyer.
Mbï yê tî tene tenne na mbênî *wandya-wakokö* / *avokäa*.

I speak English.	**I need an interpreter.**
Mbï tene Anglëe.	Mbï bezôa mbênî wagbyanngbingo-tenne.

You Might Hear

binngo-wûsûwusu disturbing the peace
karrango-ndyalêgë traffic violation
lamânde tî syonî garrengo parking fine
lamânde tî syêge lorro speeding ticket
korrongo lanngo tî vizäa overstaying your visa
nzï theft
Asï na ndo wa? Where did this happen?
Asï na ngbonga ôke? What time did it occur?
Lo yeke tôngana nye? What does he / she look like?

Cardinal Numbers

Dikkongo-wunngo

1	ôko	18	balë-ôko na *meambe* / *miombe*
2	ûse	19	balë-ôko na gümbâyä
3	otâ	20	balë-ûse
4	usyo	21	balë-ûse na ôko
5	okü	22	balë-ûse na ûse
6	omenë / omanä	30	balë-otâ
7	mbâssambala / mbrâmbrâ	31	balë-otâ na ôko
8	omeambe / meambe / miombe	32	balë-otâ na ûse
9	gümbâyä	40	balë-usyo
10	balë-ôko	50	balë-okü
11	balë-ôko na ôko	60	balë-omenë / balë-omanä
12	balë-ôko na ûse	70	balë-mbâssambala / balë-mbrâmbrâ
13	balë-ôko na otâ	80	balë-meambe / balë-miombe
14	balë-ôko na usyo	90	balë-gümbâyä
15	balë-ôko na okü	100	ngbangbo ôko
16	balë-ôko na *omenë* / *omanä*	101	ngbangbo ôko na ôko
17	balë-ôko na *mbâssambala* / *mbrâmbrâ*	200	gbangbo ûse
		500	ngbangbo okü

1,000 sâki ôko (Written with a dot in Sango: 1.000)
10,000 sâki balë-ôko
100,000 sâki ngangbo ôko
1,000,000 kûtu ôko
1,000,000,000 ngbundangbu ôko

Fractions
âfângbi-wunngo

one-quarter bêndâmbo
one-half ndâmbo
three-quarters
bêndâmbo otâ

one-third fângbitâ
two-thirds fângbitâ-ûse
all kwê
none mbênî ôko äpe

Ordinal Numbers
Dikkongo sêmolongö

first kôzo ... (nî)
second ûse ... (nî)
third otâ ... (nî)
fourth usyo ... (nî)
fifth okü ... (nî)
sixth omenë / omanä ... (nî)
seventh mbâssambala / mbrâmbrâ ... (nî)
eighth meambe / miombe ... (nî)
ninth gümbâyä ... (nî)
tenth balë-ôko ... (nî)

some (of)... kêtê gbâ tî.../ âmmbeni .../ mbâgë tî…
(a small pack of…/ some…/ a part of…)
a half ndâmbo tî…
a little kêkkete mbâgë tî…
a lot / a lot of … gbânî / gbâ tî …

more mbênî / mbênî daä	**extra small (XS)** zêgbê (Z)
less *diri* / *kiri na ngbeni*	**small (S)** sêppele (S)
enough alîngbi	**medium (M)** mbembë (M)
not enough alîngbi äpe	**large (L)** lambu (L)
too many awü ahön ndönî	**extra-large (XL)** gbâkâ (G)
too much ahön ndönî	

big kotta
bigger kotta ahön sô
biggest *kotta ahön tanga nî kwê / bêtaâ kotta … (nî)*
small kêtê
smaller kêtê ahön sô
smallest *kêtê ahön tanga nî kwê / bêtaâ kêtê …(nî)*

fat ngbobbito
skinny ngenngo
slender sêppele

wide *kotta / sai / lê sai* (big / wide / large in surface)
narrow kôfê / kpêssere / kêtê (narrow (place), narrow
(passage), small)
tall ayo na nduzzu
short ndurü
long yongôro

millimeter fâsâkimêtere
centimeter fângbangbomêtere
meter mêtere
kilometer kilomêtere / sâkimêtere

squared *sênî-ûse / karëe*
cubed *sênî-otâ / kîbi*

milliliter fâsâkilîtiri
liter lîtiri
kilogram kilöo

cup kopu
pint tögalôon / kälîsi
dame-jeanne / lady cane (20-liter bottle) damazäni
quart lîtiri
a pitcher nduttu
gallon galôon

Telling Time
Dikkongo-ngbonga

What time is it?
Ngbonga nî ayeke ôke?

It's 5 A.M.
Ayeke ngbonga 5 *tî ndäpêrê* / *tî ndën* / *kôzo na bêlâ*.

It is 5 P.M.
Ayeke ngbanga 5 tî *ndöh* / *lâkûi* / *pekô-bêlâ*

There are several ways of expressing A.M.:
tî ndäpêrê "of morning", *tî ndën* "of morning",
kôzo na bêlâ "before midday". It can be written as "ngb. 5 *ndën*" or "ngb. 5*kb*". P.M. can be expressed with *tî ndöh*, *tî lâkûi*, or *pekô-bêlâ*, written as "ngb. 5 *ndöh*" or "ngb. 5*pb*".

It's 6 o'clock.
Ayeke/ *Atï* ngbanga 6 gôh.

It's 6:30.
Ayeke ngbanga 6 na *ndâmbo* / *nzîna nî 30*.

Five past three.
Ngbanga otâ (3) na nzîna nî okü (5).

Half past two.
Ngbonga 2 na ndâmbo.

Quarter to eight.
Angbâ bêndâmbo tî sï meambe. / Angbâ nzîna ngbonga 15 tî sï ngbonga meambe.

Twenty to four.
Angbâ balë-ûse tî sï na ngbonga usyo.

noon bêlâ / bêkombïte / midy
midnight bêbï

In the ...
Na …

  morning ndäpêrê / ndën
  afternoon ndöh / pekô tî *bêlâ* / *bêkombïte*
  evening lâkûi

at night na bï
early na kotta ndapêrê / na ndatu

late (by the end of the activity) na ndângbâ nî
late (after the activity has started) na pekô-tângo
late (after the activity has finished) na pekô ni

At 1 P.M. Na ngbanga 1 *pb* / *ndöh*
At 3:28 Na ngb. 3:28

Duration

Ninngango

for ... tî ...

    one month nze ôko
    two months nze ûse
    one week *dimâsi* / *yenga* ôko
    three weeks *dimâsi* / *yenga* otâ
    one day lanngo ôko
    four days lanngo usyo
    one hour ngbonga ôko
    a half hour ndâmbo tî ngbonga ôko
    one minute nzîna ngbonga ôko
    five minutes nzîna ngbonga okü
    one second yakerre ngbonga ôko
    five seconds yakerre ngbonga okü

since ngbêreyê / dipîi
during *na ndembë tî...* (*Require a noun as complement)
       sô... (*Require a sentence as complement)
before *kôzonî na ...* / *kôzo* / *tî kôzo*
after na pekô *tî... / nî*

one year ago *asâra ngû ôko* / *ngû ôko kôzonî*
five years ago *asâra ngû okü* / *ngû okü kôzonî*

six months ago *asâra nze omenë* / *nze omenë kôzonî*

in two years na ngû ûse
in five months na nze okü
in two weeks na *dimâsi / yenga* ûse
in twelve days na lanngo balë-ôko na ûse
in three hours na ngbonga otâ
in five minutes na nzîna ngbonga okü
in ten seconds na yakerre ngbonga balë-ôko

Stating the Date
Fanngo-kâpä

yesterday bîrï	**week** dimâsi / yenga
today lâsô	**month** nze
tomorrow kêkerêke	**year** ngû

this week (na) dimâsi sô
next week (na) dimâsi tî pekô
last week (na) dimâsi sô ahön sô

this month (na) nze sô
next month (na) nze tî pekô
last month (na) *nze tî kôzo / nze sô ahön sô*

this year (na) ngû sô
next year (na) ngû tî pekô
last year (na) *ngû tî kôzo / ngû sô ahön sô*

Days of the Week
Âlanngo tî *dimâsi/yenga*

Monday Bikua-ôko	Saturday Lâpôso
Tuesday Bikua-ûse	Sunday Lâyenga
Wednesday Bikua-otâ	
Thursday Bikua-usyo	
Friday Bikua-okü	

Months of the Year
Ânze tî ngû ôko

January Nyenye	July Lengua
February Fulundïgi	August Kukkuru
March Mbanngu	September Mvuka
April Ngubë	October Ngberere
May Bêlawwu	November Nabanndüru
June Föndo	December Kakawuka

Seasons
Ângoi

Winter Burüdê
Spring Konndoko
Summer Zonngo / Ngûnzapä
Fall/Autumn Ndorokugbë

dry season Burü
rainy/wet season Ngûnzapä / Zonngo

Countries
Âkoddoro

Australia Osotraly
Belgium Belezîki / Bêleze
Canada Kanadäa
China Syîni
England Angletëre
France Farânzi
Germany Zâmani
India Ênde / Hîndi
Ireland Irrilânde
New Zealand Finî-Zelânde
Scotland Ekôsi
Spain Espânye
Portugal Pûra / Koddoro Pûra
United Kingdom Koddorogbya-ôko (tî Angletëre)
United States of America Âkanza koddoro tî Amerîka

African Countries
Âkoddoro tî afrîka

Algeria Alazery
Angola Angoläa
Benin Benëen
Burkina Faso Burkina Faso
Burundi Burundi
Cameroon Kamerûne
Chad Tyâde

Central African Republic Koddorosêse tî Bêafrîka / Bêafrîka

Congo (The Republic of) Kongö (Koddorosêse tî)

Congo (The Democratic Republic of the) Kongö (Koddorosêse tî Ngunuhalëzo tî)

Egypt Ezîpiti

Eritrea Eritrëe

Ethiopia Etiopy

Eswatini Eswatîni

Gabon Gaböon

Gambia Gambï

Equatorial Guinea Ginëe tî Ekuatëre

Guinea / Guinea-Conakry Ginëe / Ginëe-Konakîrî

Guinea-Bisau Ginëe-Biso / Ginëe-Bisau

Lesotho Lesôto

Liberia Liberïa

Madagascar Madagasikära

Mali Maly

Mauritania Moritany

Mauritius Mörîsi

Morocco Marôko

Namibia Namiby

Niger Nizëre

Nigeria Nizerïa

Rwanda Ruandäa

Senegal Senegäle

Saychelles Seysyêle

Sierra Leone Sierra Leöne

Somalia Somaly

South Africa Afrîka-Mbongo / Afrîka tî Mbongo

Sudan Sudäan
Southern Sudan Sudäan tî Mbongo
Tunisia Tunizy
Togo Togöo
Zambia Zamby
Zimbabwe Zimbabwe

CITIES
Âgbatta

Saango pronunciations provided in brackets.

United States of America
Âkanza koddoro tî Amerîka

Boston [bôstoni]
Chicago [shikagöo]
Dallas [dalâsa]
Los Angeles [lôs andielêsi]
Philadelphia [filadelfii]
New York [nû-yôrke]
Washington, D.C. [wasyingïton]

Canada
Kanadäa

Quebec [kebêke]
Toronto [torontöo]
Vancouver [vankûvere]

European Union
Kunndu koddoro tî Potto

Berlin [berlëen]
Dublin [dublëen]
London [lôndono / lôndro]
Paris [pary]

Africa
Afrîka

Abuja [abûdia]
Asmara [asmara]
Bamako [bamako]
Banjul [bandyûlu]
Bangui [bangî]
Brazzaville [brazawîli]
Bujumbura [buzumbura]
Cairo [kêre]
Cotonou [kotonu]
Dakar [dakar/ndakâru]
Dodoma [dodoma]
Dar-es-Salam
[dar-es-salam]
Harare [Harare]
Johannesbourg
[dyohannesbûru]
Kigali [kigäli]

Kinshasa [kinsasa /
kinshasa]
Libreville [lîbrawîli]
Lilongwe [Lilongwe]
Luanda [Luanda]
Lomé [lomë]
Maputo [maputo]
Mbata [mbata]
Monrovia [monrovia]
Nairobi [nairoby]
Ndjamena [ndiamêna]
Niamey [nyamë]
Maseru [maseru]
Mbabane [mbabâne]
Rabat [rabäa]
Tunis [tunîsi]
Windoeck [wïndûku]